WINNING AT THE CARD GAME OF LIFE

WINNING AT THE CARD GAME OF LIFE

Success Depends Not Upon the Cards You Were Dealt, but rather How You Play Them.

BOB MCGLENN, PH.D.

To order additional copies of this book, contact:
Xlibris Corporation
1-888-795-4274
www.Xlibris.com
Orders@Xlibris.com
56667

CONTENTS

DEDICATION

To the greatest hand ever dealt, my family,
who bring love, support, and meaning to my life.

PREFACE

Success depends not upon the cards you were dealt,
but rather how you play them.

Christine had anything but a perfect childhood. Her father was an alcoholic and abusive. As a small child, she didn't know why her father would come into her room at night and touch her in ways that made her feel so dirty. She was afraid to tell her mother because of the daily beatings that she and her younger sister feared might occur. "Mom must have known, but what could she do. He would only beat her too." Christine found refuge in going to school. There, she could feel safe. There, no one beat you. There, you were listened to. There, you do more than just dream that there was a better life. As she entered high school, Christine had started to find her voice. One night she told her father that never more would he be allowed to touch her. And if she learned he had touched her younger sisters, she would kill him. Christine started working after school and moved out as soon as she graduated. She worked full-time and went to school at the community college. She went on to study business at the local university and, in a few years, found herself managing and owning her own restaurant. Today she is happily married with three beautiful and happy children.

Brad had it all, good looks, intelligence, and money. In the small town in which Brad grew, up his family was considered to be rich. His father was a successful banker, and his mother knew all the right people and was active in all the most prominent charities. Being an only child, Brad didn't lack for attention or toys. He had just about whatever he or his friends could imagine. In high school, he had the newest and fastest car. And when that car earned him a ticket, he somehow didn't have to go to traffic school. Brad dated the prettiest girls, taking them to the coolest places and getting whatever he wanted from them. Despite being out late and never turning in homework, Brad always seemed to pass his classes. Beer, drugs, anything he desired seemed to come his way. One day, the golden goose of life seemed to stop providing for Brad. After totaling his third car and flunking out of college, his parents stopped supporting him and cleaning up his mistakes. Feeling that he was entitled to earning more than a minimum wage, he found few employers interested in him, and those jobs he did get, he would quickly lose. Today Brad is living in a homeless shelter and begging for quarters.

Frank was a gifted high school athlete and student who came from a loving family. He was popular and respected by all that knew him. His future shone bright with scholarships and dreams until that one piercing moment in time when a drunk driver crossed the center of the road and plowed into Frank's car. Frank was alive, but barely. As the rescue workers cut him from the twisted metal, it was not clear what part of him was not broken or damaged. After hours of surgery and days of waiting, the outcome was clearer. Frank would live, but he would never walk again. His days of running across the football field before cheering crowds were over. Now the issue was not where he would go to college, but rather if he would go to college. With the support of his family and friends and his own determination, Frank embarked on the long road to recovery. He never walked again, but he did compete athletically again, in the wheelchair games. He went on to get his degree, start his own business, and today is married with two children.

Christine, Brad, and Frank were each dealt a different hand of cards in life. How Christine and Frank played their cards led to them being successful, while Brad wasted the hand he was dealt. Some may say it was a matter of luck what happened to these people. Such people may say, "Sure, they had something to do with the outcomes of their lives, but it was luck that determined the final outcome." There is a saying:

Luck is the residue of design.

There is no luck in one person choosing the path of education and the other the path of drug abuse. There is no luck in one person maximizing what they have and another wasting what they had. Luck does not lead to success; success is the product of a design.

I was watching TV one evening and came upon a story about two women who knew something about luck and gambling. These women lived in Las Vegas. By day, they were the typical soccer moms: driving kids around, cleaning house, baking cookies. They were devoted to their families, and it showed in the healthy way they all interacted. By night, after putting the kids to bed, these women would drive to the casinos for a night of playing poker. But they didn't just play poker—they won at poker. They didn't win every night, but over the course of the month, they would always come out way ahead, thousands of dollars ahead. They won so much money that they had paid off their homes and cars and had built up a very nice savings. How did they do it? In poker, you don't always get the best cards, but these women knew how to best play those cards so that over time, they would come out ahead. Life is like that. We do not always have control over the cards we are dealt, but it is our choice on how we play them. We do not have control over earthquakes or fires or the death of loved ones or car accidents. There are many things in life that occur that may take everything from us, except for how we react. At such times many, people find comfort in saying, "Things work out for the best." I have always had trouble with that saying. How can you say that it is best for a child to die in a school shooting or for hundred of thousands of people to parish in a tsunami? What is best about these tragedies? I do not believe that "things work out for the best," but rather, we make the best out of what works out. In life, you may not be dealt the best looks, the most talent, or the greatest parents, but how do you direct your life in a way to get the most out of what you have? What moves do you make to get better use out of the cards you were dealt so you can get further down the road to success?

For over thirty years, I have worked as a clinical psychologist. I have worked in all levels of schools as a school psychologist, worked in hospitals training interns, worked with the homeless, and established and ran a trauma unit on a high school campus after a school shooting. My experience has been broad, and I've had the privilege of being invited into the lives of many people in crisis. I have witnessed firsthand the human qualities in action that led to happiness and those that hindered recovery. I have seen what it takes to be successful and the difficult and very individualized journey it takes to get there. I have spoken with young adults seeking ways to find their road to success. They search for the ingredients that lie in successful people and how they too might gain those qualities. Everyone wants to be successful because "If I'm successful, I will be happy." While this may appear to be a simplistic statement, it is also a very accurate statement. The key word that needs to be explored and defined is *success*. What is success? Is it different for different people? Is it possible that everyone be successful? It is at this point that I decided to start my journey of writing this book.

My original plan for the book was to interview successful people from all walks of life. Men and women from diverse backgrounds who, when faced with a variety of obstacles and blessings, played their cards well enough to arrive at a level of success. The people I interviewed are not famous so that you would quickly recognize their names, but what they have achieved lifts them beyond famous to special. They have become the best that they can be and serve as an example of the best that potentially lies in each of us. They would be quick to tell you that their lives are not special or heroic, nor are they successful at everything they do. All they did was to play the best they could the cards they were dealt against antagonists not of their choosing. They are not perfect human beings; they are the reflection of the perfection that can lie in human beings. They are role models of what we can become. Charles Barkley, a former professional basketball player once said that he was not a role model for anyone. He was wrong. We are all role models. It's just a question of what kind of role model you will be. The men and women whose stories are related in this book are role models of the highest order. Their stories provide a glimpse into what it takes to be successful and provide inspiration for each of us to play our cards that much better.

While conducting the interviews, I started to observe some common characteristics or factors in their stories that contributed to their being successful. I found what it takes to be successful was best described in a simple acronyms I created called CARDS. But having worked for all of my professional life with people seeking a better direction in their life, I realized I couldn't just tell someone what they need; I had to show them how to get it. It's one thing to tell someone that eating fish is good for them, but it does no good if you don't show them how to fish. So this book has evolved from presenting role models to what it takes and how to become those role models yourself. While writing the book, I spoke to high school classes about CARDS and tried out some of the exercises you will find in the book. I have been told by teachers that CARDS gave their students new belief in their potential to succeed and the tools to do so. I have students, years after graduating, telling me that when reflecting on high school, what they remembered the most was CARDS, which they still use to guide their life. This led to the section in the book for using CARDS in the classroom.

I have a basic belief that everyone can be successful. You can be successful if you choose to take the journey. I have confidence that you will find this book helpful in your journey to success no matter what stage in the process you find yourself. And I hope you too will come to realize that everyone can be successful. For me personally, my journey to success has been filled with questions about what is success and am I doing enough to fulfill my destiny. I have been dealt some cards that aren't too good, and I have been blessed with some very high cards.

Yet I have found solace in realizing that winning at the card game of life does not depend upon the final out come, but rather how I go about getting there. Success truly does not depend upon the cards you were dealt, but rather how you play them. You can achieve your dreams. You can feel the peace that comes from respecting yourself. You can feel the sense of confidence that comes with knowing that you are successful. You only have to be willing to pick up your cards and learn how best to play them in the card game of life.

Acknowledgments

No author writes a book, especially a self-help book, without getting a whole lot of help.

First, I am indebted to the men and women who allowed me to share their stories. They are all extraordinary people who epitomize not only what is success, but also what is best about humanity. Their life stories serve to educate and inspire all of us on our journey to success.

Second, I want to thank Jonathan LeMaster, Bill Madigan, Frank Patrick, Bob Heveron, and Marcia Reiss-Franklin who served as editors and mentors to me in my journey writing this book. Being able to bounce ideas off them and to learn from their suggestions was invaluable. I'm especially grateful to Marcia not only for her gift as a writer, but more so for her constant support, encouragement, and belief in the book.

Third, I am grateful to Brittany Doan, whose artwork on the cover creatively captured what the book portrayed, and to Jonathan Gardner, whose graphic art skills made it happen.

Finally, saying thank you is not enough for the love and support I receive daily from my wife, Diana, my children Jennifer, Matthew, and Michael, and son-in-law, Jonathan. If I finished the book or not, they give me the kind of love and support that is unconditional and constant, while communicating a belief in me that brings the best out of me.

The Keys to Success are in the Cards

As I interviewed people who were successful, I started to question, "What is it that has gone into their being successful?" What is it about successful people or about what they have done that led to their achieving success? If success is the result of how you play the cards you were dealt, then maybe what it takes to be successful is also found in the cards. As I explored that concept further, I concluded that in fact, there are five basic common factors found in all successful people, and these factors are hidden in the cards.

All Successful People Have a Scheme.

A *scheme* is a plan, a blueprint, a map of what you want to achieve. Successful people know where they want to go, and they have a clear idea of how to get there. You would not start to bake a dessert without knowing what you wanted to make and what the recipe was. A pilot would not take off without having a flight plan and a destination. So why do people embark on life without some idea of where they want to go? And yet, many times, we do not know what it is we are trying to accomplish; we just react to what happens. If we are not a stimulus in life with a direction and purpose, we are just a response to whatever happens to us. Successful people are stimuli. They make things happen. They know what they want and what they must do to achieve it. Successful people have and set goals.

It could be argued that most everyone has goals for their life, but successful people know how to set successful goals. That is the difference. Many times, we set goals but do not recognize how the goal has the potential to fail before any attempt to pursue it. How to set goals that do not have the potential of blowing-up in one's face is crucial to achieving one's goal. To make a potentially successful goal five ingredients in the goal must first be identified.

1. *It must be **definable***. Can you put the goal into words? If you cannot make the goal understandable, then how can you identify what is the first step and each step to follow? The process of defining the goal is crucial to creating the map to the final destination.
2. *It must be **achievable***. Is the goal something that lies within your given strengths and abilities? I could say that my goal is to play center in the NBA, but I am over fifty years old, I'm barely six feet tall, and I can't jump high. If I made this goal for myself, I would be doomed to failure before I got started.
3. *It must be **desirable***. Is the goal something that you really want to do? Is it something that you really want to achieve, not something you feel you should do? I had a coworker who shared the story that his father always wanted him to be a lawyer. He didn't want to be a lawyer, but he followed his father's desires and went to Berkeley Law School with the intent of flunking out his final year. To his surprise, due the riots at Berkeley, everyone was graduated early. So he went on and failed the bar exam twice and then did what he wanted to do, which was to become a psychologist. He had achieved a very difficult goal. He had graduated from a prestigious law school, but his success had no joy because it was not what he desired to do with his life.
4. *It must be **measurable***. Have you stated how long and what quantity is necessary for you to achieve the goal? If you cannot measure your goal, then how do you know if you have achieved it? I hear people say that their goal is to be happy. Being happy is certainly a very good goal to have, but how will you know when you are happy? When asked about when they will know they are happy, the conversation usually goes something like this:

> "It's a feeling, I'll know the feeling."

> Then I usually reply as any smart-aleck psychologist would. "How do you know what you feel is happiness? Maybe it's gas." Before I can get the full impact of their look of disgust or confusion, I usually ask, "What makes you happy?"

> "I like to jog, jogging makes me happy."

> "How many times a week must you jog to be happy?"

"Three times a week."

"So if you jog three times per week, then you are happy."

"Yes, being able to jog three times per week makes me happy."

When stated this way, the goal of happiness is now not only definable, but it is measurable as well. By being measurable, the goal setter knows when they achieved it. The same applies to any goal you set. By stating that you will read twenty (quantity) pages by three o'clock next Monday (time), you have established a goal that has a targeted end point.

5. *It must be **controllable**.* Do you have power over everything and everyone in your stated goal? I can state that my goal is "to have dinner at the Red Lobster next Friday at 8:00 with my wife." My goal is certainly definable—dinner at the Red Lobster. It is achievable—I'm off work at that time, and I can get there. It is desirable—I like eating there, and I love being with my wife. It is measurable—next Friday at 8:00. It is *not* controllable. I do not have control over my wife. I never have and never will! She may say that she is busy that night or she would like to go somewhere else. As my goal is stated now, her not going means I did not achieve my goal and I failed. I literally failed before I left home. But if I worded the goal as "I will *ask* my wife to have dinner with me at the Red Lobster next Friday at 8:00" I can succeed. I have control over the *asking* not over someone else *doing*. This is where the majority of goals fail. They are designed in such a way that to achieve success depends upon what someone else does. Many couples I see have trouble in their relationship because they have set their goal and their sense of self-worth on making their partner happy. You cannot make another person happy. Your goal can be to contribute to the opportunities for your partner to be happy, but you cannot force them or will them to be happy. Each person must make himself or herself happy.

Therefore, the first step in making a scheme or plan is to create potentially successful goals, yet a scheme can provide more than just direction, it can be a source of motivation as well. This is done through the power of visualization.

Visualization is what you see the Olympic gymnasts due before they start their routine. They are rehearsing their performance in their mind and throughout their body before performing it. They are rehearsing success. I had a figure skater come to me because she was having trouble passing her qualifying standards to the next level of competition. She was a dedicated skater who practiced long hours in the pursuit of perfecting her technique, yet when it came time to perform, she would trip or fall. As I talked with her, it became evident that she could identify very clearly what she was doing wrong. She talked about the angle of her skate the balance that was thrown off by her arm position, and on and on she spoke about what she had done wrong. It soon became evident to me that she had analyzed her performances so much that she had been rehearsing failure. All that went through her mind was how she had failed and what she didn't want to do again. She was thinking the opposite of what she needed to have running through her mind. She needed to focus on how to do it right, not how to fail. So I hypnotized her and had her imagine that as she stepped onto the ice, she could feel the power of the ice come flowing up through her skates; she felt at one with the music, and most importantly, she experienced the flawless performance of her routine. Since I would be seeing this skater only once, we recorded the visualization session so she could listen to it at home. And listen to it she did. Three times a day, she would either listen to the tape or imagine the session on her own. Three weeks later, I got a phone call. She had passed her qualifying. Her coach said that he had never seen her skate with such strength and confidence. And by the way, she had the flu when she did it. This young skater had visualized her success and then achieved it.

How often in life do you hear someone criticizing themselves? "I'm too fat," "I'm too klutzy," "I'm not smart enough," or "I'm not a good mother." We hear such things all of the time, and it's not that they want to be these things. In fact, they would like to be the opposite, but as long as they refer to themselves in this manner, they will only solidify further their being just that. This is due to the "genie" in our unconscious. This genie will give us just about whatever we ask for; the problem is the words we use to ask for it. Let me give you an example of what I'm driving at. Right now, I do not want you to think of an elephant. OK, what color was it? You saw, maybe for a moment, an image of an elephant. You couldn't help yourself. That is because we think in picture words. Words that generate pictures create images in our minds, and it is these images that the genie responds to. Qualifiers such as "do not" have no affect on the picture generated; thus, the genie responds only to the picture. When you say, "I do not want to be fat," the words "do not" don't register, so the genie is commanded, "I want to be fat." If you say, "I do not want to fail this test," the image that is being rehearsed in your mind is of you failing the test. What you need to say is, "I will get an A on the test or I will be relaxed and the information and answers will just flow from me." If you don't believe in the power of visualization, just walk into a room of seven-year-old boys and tell them to stop acting like monkeys. I will guarantee you that at least one of them will start making noises and acting like a monkey. The image of being a monkey is too powerful, and the impulse to act is too strong to do other than to behave like a monkey. Skilled teachers have learned that the best way to calm down a class is to be calm, speak in a calm manner, and illicit calming images in their students. We become what we visualize and are products of our visions.

As I stated earlier, visualization is an important part of your scheme. The more detailed your vision of your goal, the more powerful will be the drive to achieve it. If you can imagine yourself already succeeding and know how it will feel, the greater will be the pull to get there. You will start to believe that you belong there. You will get comfortable with your destination and will become more excited to reach it. Your next task would then be to visualize each step you will need to take to accomplish your goal. It is a good idea to not only visualize each step, but to also write it down. Again, in as much detail as possible. The more detail, the more alive it will become.

Let us imagine that your goal is to build a backyard patio with a barbeque. You can visualize the design and shape of the patio. You can identify the type of barbeque you want and where it is located. This provides you with a picture of what you want, your primary goal. But this is not the only goal that needs to be reached. You have to break that picture down into smaller steps or goals that need to be reached. For example, you have to decide on the materials to be used, the exact dimensions of the patio, who is going to build it, and how are you going to pay for it. Each of those goals can be broken down into smaller goals, such as for materials you might have, as a goal to identify the price of various materials to choose between and where to get them. With each goal, there is a smaller goal behind it that has to be completed before you can move on. Once you have reached what appears to be the starting goal, you then follow the ladder of goals until the patio and barbeque is completed, one step at a time. Too often people don't clearly identify all the steps involved, or they try to skip steps along the way. This may get you offtrack, slow down progress, and contribute to you getting discouraged and giving up. Focusing on the smaller steps keeps the over all task from feeling too large and overwhelming. The same holds true when charting your direction in life.

All Successful People Know How to Make Good Decisions.

While it may be obvious that successful people make good decisions, it is the process of making decisions that is not always so clear. For example, if you were to buy one hundred shares of a stock at $10 a share and it then sky rocketed to being worth $1,000 a share you would now have $1 million. Such a decision would be termed as successful. But the key to this success lies in how the decision was made to choose the stock, which has more to it than just getting lucky.

You make decisions all of the time. You decide when to get up in the morning. You decide what to eat. You decide to go to work or not. You decide to talk or not. You decide to go home or not. You make thousands of decisions every day. You have even decided to read this book. We make so many decisions that we don't even notice that they are being made. Because of the volume of decisions we make, many people lose track of their power to make decisions; they feel they have no choice. Such people will tell you, "I have to get up now" or "I have to go to work" or "I have to put up with the abuse." In fact, you could decide to stay in bed and not go to work, but the consequences of such actions are more than you want to experience, so you get up and go to work. Every decision has a consequence attached to it, and successful people take that into consideration before making their decision.

There are basically three golden rules of behavior. The first, "No one does anything they don't want to do." Oh, we may not like the choices, but we do what we do because we choose to do it. The second, "Everything we do makes sense at the time that we do it." Now, what we do may not make sense later or make sense to others who are watching us, but in that time and space, it makes logical, rational sense to us under the circumstances. The third, "We do what we do because the advantages outweigh the disadvantages." We believe that we will gain more from what we are doing than if we did not do it. Where a problem emerges is when a particular behavior that proved to be successful in the past no longer brings successful results, yet we still keep acting the same way. In other words, the advantages no longer exist, but we keep doing it. For example, a child who lives under the threat of being beaten would learn to be submissive and to avoid conflict. As an adult, this same person may have problems at work or in a relationship because they are reluctant to speak up and express their needs or point of view. There were very clear advantages to keeping quiet as a child, but as an adult, the advantages no longer exist, and being passive only leads to more problems. In such cases, the person has to stop and decide if the advantages still exist or if they should make a new decision on how to behave. Successful people recognize that life is a series of adjustments that are made based upon the ever-changing advantages and disadvantages. Those who are resilient enough to adjust become successful.

If you were to ask a successful person why they made a particular decision, they may say that they didn't think about it, they just did it, but that would not be entirely true. Successful people are analyzing the logic behind their actions before they move; nothing is decided on a whim. The thought process may have been done long before the action and had become so integrated into the person that they might refer to their actions as being the result of intuition and not a conscious decision. But in fact, it was a conscious decision that had been thought out at some earlier place and time that when repeatedly reinforced over time, had melded into intuition. It is the unsuccessful people who act impulsively and find themselves trapped, going nowhere. Such people often start to blame others for their situation. "You made me do it." "You made me say it." "I can't because they won't let me." By such people not taking responsibility for their own behavior, they are giving up their basic power as a human being, the power to decide. Remember the three golden rules of behavior. You always have the power to decide, even if you don't have control over your choices. An employee may have an abusive, demanding boss, but they can't leave the job because they need the money. While they cannot control or change their situation, they can control their response to the situation. They can decide to not take personally what the boss says and work to find pleasure and fulfillment elsewhere. A colleague of mine, Dr. Mark Katz, spent years working with extremely emotionally disturbed children who lived in very dysfunctional families. He worried about what would be their future given such emotional problems. When he sought out these children as adults, he was surprised to find that a vast majority were doing very well. The problems they were having as children no longer existed. Dr. Katz concluded that when they were children, they could not escape their living situation; they were trapped. As adults, if in a dysfunctional situation, they had the power to decide to leave. You can escape the abuse and make a decision to do what is best for you. You can make a decision to change your life.

Jennifer's life was changed by a decision she made. At age four, Jennifer was adopted by a couple who thought that having a child would save their marriage. By age seven, the couple was divorcing, and custody of Jennifer was awarded to her mother because her father was an alcoholic. Her mother wasn't much better. She was abusive to Jennifer. Her idea of teaching her daughter about fire was to try to put her hand in fire. Jennifer had many chores around the house, and if the floor had not been scrubbed to her mother's satisfaction, Jennifer would be beaten. By age twelve, Jennifer had contracted a severe eating disorder resulting in hospitalization. She also acted out to the point that she was removed from her home and became a ward of the court. She was placed in foster homes and group homes, but everywhere she went, she would run away and cause trouble. By age sixteen, her father had been sober for two years and had remarried. Jennifer went to live with him, his new wife, and her two daughters, which were about Jennifer's age. Things did not go smoothly, and one day, Jennifer asked her father why he never supported her whenever there was a conflict. He stated that he couldn't side with her because he had a good thing going and he didn't want to blow it. This angered and hurt Jennifer, so she went to her room and took all of her antidepressant pills. She was in intensive care for three days and probably should have died given the number of pills she took and the toxic levels in her system, but she did not die. As she lay recovering in her hospital room, her family doctor came in and sat beside her and said, "Jenny, you have a decision to make. You have the rest of your life before you. What are you going to do with it? Are you going to keep looking backward for something that you will never find, or are you going to go forward and make your own happiness?"

Something in what he said turned on a switch in her head, and Jennifer decided to take charge of her life. She went back to high school and graduated early. She got a scholarship to the University of Wisconsin and studied science. She became a registered nurse and is now a trauma nurse in a local hospital and a flight nurse and captain in the United States Air Force Reserve. Most importantly, she is a mentally healthy, positive person who is capable of maintaining stable and trusting relationships. Jennifer took her power to decide and made a decision to take charge of her life and turn it around. She could have easily succumbed to the dysfunction around her, but she did not. The right words at the right time stirred her to decide to take action. This is what successful people do. They decide to take charge of their own lives and never turn back.

Decisions such as the one Jennifer made or any decision to change is not made just once, but rather must be made over and over again. If someone decides to lose weight, they must make that same decision each time they eat anything. They must decide whether what they are about to eat will contribute to their goal of losing weight. Every student will say they want to make straight As, but how many make the decisions to do what it takes to make an A in a course? The A student decides to spend time studying, to review what they have learned, to listen in class, to complete all assignments. A good student decides to make school a priority in their life, and other things that take their time are secondary. It is like having a big rock in the middle of the stream, and the water has to flow around it. To a good student, the rock is school, and the water is the rest of their life, which must flow around the immovable object. School cannot be the only rock in one's stream. There may be other rocks—such as family, integrity, and honesty—because these are the constants upon which we define our lives. Such constants are found in the lives of successful people, and it is clear that they have decided to keep them in their lives.

Successful people decide to make decisions that are positive and life enhancing, not destructive and self-defeating. They stay away from those situations that will not contribute to reaching their goals or ruin their chances of success. They stay away form substance abuse and people that would only lead their journey in a direction of failure. That is not to say that successful people have not gone down such roads, because many have. What is different with these people is that they quickly learned from their mistakes and decided to apply the self-discipline needed to go in another direction. They decided to take charge of their own life, their own destiny.

All Successful People Know How to Use Available Resources.

The *New World Dictionary of American English* defines *resources* as "something that lies ready for use or that can be drawn upon for aid or to take care of a need ... applies to any person, thing, action, etc. to which one turns for aid in time of need or emergency."

If you were stranded on an island, you would use what was available to you to ensure your survival. You would use the resources around you to create a shelter so you could be protected, to start a signal fire so you could be rescued, and to provide food so you can eat. It would be nice to be able to call for room service, but on a deserted island, there is no such resource. You have to use what is available to you. The same can be said for life. We have resources all around us: the telephone, the Internet, friends, and family. We often take such things for granted, yet they are resources that if used properly, can contribute to our being successful. Successful people seek out and utilize the resources that are available to them. They foster relationships with people who have knowledge to give and support to render. They are open to finding those people and information that will help them on their quest to reach a goal. They are also alert to resources that may suddenly be available that could have a profound influence on their lives. Events, people, or opportunities may cross one's path that will totally alter the course of their life. The obvious events are things like accidents that might change one's physical state or perception of the fragility of life. Yet there are also more subtle opportunities, such as being asked to watch someone's dog for the summer and you find you love working with animals. Maybe a teacher asks you to help another student and you find you love teaching. Maybe someone takes an interest in you and you find you want to be just like them. Sometimes from such resources come our passions.

In addition to the resources all around us, there are those within us. A successful person has discovered what talents, skills, and interests lie within them, and they then develop those resources. This takes a considerable amount of honesty. I may think it would be great to sing before thousands at Carnegie Hall, but if carrying a tune is not a resource I possess, then there may be a problem. The United States Constitution says we are all created equal, but if you have heard me sing, then you know that this is not true. We all have different abilities. We may all have equal rights, but we are not all equal. And it is good that we are not. The inequality between us is what makes us unique and life interesting. Finding our talents and then pursing them is what successful people do. What is fortunate is that by asking what interests you, you will find a major clue of where your talents lie. By nature, we most often do that which is most reinforcing to us. Ray Charles didn't play the piano because he had to; he played the piano because he liked doing it, and he liked doing it because he had the talent to do it. You may have many talents, and it is hard to identify the central ones. But your future may actually lie in the combination of those talents. Again, honesty is important in assessing one's talents. You may have a real interest in science and be very good at analyzing information, but if you can't stand being around sick people, then becoming a doctor is not advised. You may want to direct your talents in another area of science.

People who blend the resources within them with the resources around them are one big step farther down the road to success.

All Successful People Maintain a Positive Attitude.

Successful people have a perception of life that actually goes beyond being positive and has more to do with how they define *success* and *failure*. This attitude was clearly portrayed in the movie *Apollo 13*. This is the true story of the American mission to the moon upon which everything seemed to go wrong. There was an explosion while in flight, systems malfunctioned, and landing on the moon had to be aborted. As the three astronauts ran out of fuel, it seemed it would be impossible to return them to earth alive. There is a scene in the movie where a large group of engineers were meeting to determine what could be done to rescue the crew. After sharing with them the gravity of the situation, the mission director challenged them to find a solution. As he started to leave the room, he stated that they were to explore every option and to remember, "Failure is not an option." To successful people, failure is not an option; they have no concept of failure. There is the story of when Thomas Edison was first presenting his new invention, the electric lightbulb, to the media. During the course of the presentation, it came out that there had been over two thousand experiments that had failed. When asked how it felt to have failed two thousand times, Edison's reply was "I did not fail two thousand times, it took two thousand steps to invent the lightbulb." Vince Lombardi reportedly once said that he never lost a football game; he just ran out of time. Successful people do not have the concept of failure. To them, there is no such thing as failure. If something didn't lead to the results that they desired, then they would just have to get there in another way. To successful people, they may not have won the game, but they never failed at the game. To them, failure means being done, stopped, or finished; and since they never see themselves as being finished, moving forward, and meeting the challenges in life, they will never reach a point of failure.

Imagine what your life would be like if you eliminated the concept of failure. There would be no more worrying about how well you did on a test or if that special someone really does love you. You would know that whatever happens, there would be tomorrow, and you would move forward. The fear of failure has paralyzed many a person from even attempting to achieve success. It has kept athletes from reaching their potential and students from accessing the information in their memory to pass the test. People who are afraid of failing are tight in their thinking and actions. They are afraid to take the risks to learn something new or to go further in their careers. Instead, they stay frozen wishing they had more, but fearing to go for it. Such focus on the negative only increases the likelihood of failing. Why is it that an immigrant to our country is four times more likely to become a millionaire than an American-born? It is because they operate under the basic premise that they can make it? Successful people know they will make it. They may not know when or how, but they know they will make it. They do not give themselves the option of failing. I have seen too many students who say they want to be successful but give themselves the permission to fail. They give themselves permission to not turn in all of their homework or go to all of their classes. When you give yourself such permission to do less than your all, you are accepting failure as an option. If doing all of your homework and attending all of your classes is the only option, then you are saying that succeeding is your only goal. The attitude of successful people is that "failure is not an option, and success is the only option."

All Successful People Define Their Lives by Their Commitment.

To be committed to something is to have a passion for it. We hear it often said at high school graduations for the young graduates to find what they are passionate about and to dedicate their lives to the pursuit of it. In other words, find what floats your boat and go for a sail. What is it that excites you, that brings purpose in your life, that makes you want to get out of bed in the morning? Successful people have found what they are passionate about and have committed their life to the pursuit of it. It fills their life with purpose and meaning, and it serves as the magnet that pulls them forward in life. I once had the honor of taking a graduate class from Dr. Viktor Frankl. Dr. Frankl was a survivor of the Auschwitz concentration camp during World War II, and upon his release, he presented the principles of logotherapy in his book *Man's Search for Meaning*. In the book and in the class, he spoke of having lost loved ones to the Nazi gas chambers as well as his being stripped of every worldly possession. On the finals for the course, there was only one question, and he expected us to answer it just as he had related the answer. The question was "Man finds meaning when . . ." And the answer was "when he invests himself in someone or something beyond himself." That investment could be in one's family, in a job, or in a cause. Whatever it is, when you invest yourself in someone or something beyond yourself, you will find the meaning of your life.

As you search your life experiences, interests, and desires, you may find that you have more than one passion to which you are committed. You may feel a commitment and passion to get the best for your family. You may feel a commitment to creating new and positive products at your job. You may feel a commitment as a fan to your sports team. Each of our passions has a differing level of importance, which may change over time. As children get older and move out, our commitment to them may still be present, but it takes another form. Events and needs may dictate how and if we pursue our passion. It is hard to pursue your passion to write poetry when you don't have food to eat. At the other end of the financial spectrum, you may feel trapped in a job by the "golden handcuffs" of all of the money you are making. It is hard to leave security for the uncertainty of a passion. Yet for some, acting on achieving their goal is not an option; it is a necessity. For those facing terminal illness such as Moira Podgurski, fighting for her passion is a matter of life and death.

Moira had known the challenges of setting goals and fighting to reach them having been a world-class hurdler and model in her younger days. As a mother of three children ranging in age of one and a half to seven years and married to a devoted husband, Moira felt she had all that was truly important in life until December 23, 1986. That was the day a doctor told her that she had leukemia and gave her two to five years to live. She was more than devastated. It was as if a beautiful symphony had suddenly stopped, and there was only dark silence. Who switched her world from idyllic to that of total pain and fear? She wanted to live. She wanted to raise her young children. She wanted to see them graduate and get married and have their own lives. This was her life, and she wanted it back. She was not ready to lie down and die. She had to live for them. Despite what her doctors said about putting her affairs in order, she researched every known treatment of leukemia. On the urging of some friends, she and her husband flew to the M. D. Anderson clinic in Houston in an attempt to talk her way into a clinical trial to test the drug interferon and its effects on leukemia. She was very convincing and was accepted into the trial. She was placed in a group that would be on interferon therapy alone while others in the study would have interferon plus aggressive radiation as their therapy. Each day that her husband injected the interferon into her muscles, she would get deathly sick. For the next ten years, she would feel like she had the worst flu imaginable, but she kept going. She had to keep going for her kids and husband. Each day, she would exercise, maintain a strict healthy diet, and, above all, be positive. Even when at her worse, she would look at her children and shake herself out of the negative thoughts and move on, caring for them. It has been over twenty years since Moira was diagnosed with leukemia. She as been off the interferon for years, and her doctors can't explain it, but she is totally cancer free and the only subject in the clinical trial who survived. You can say it was the drug that saved her life, and it probably was a big factor, but for those of us who know Moira, we know it was something else. She had made a commitment to do whatever it took to survive for her family. She developed a scheme of what to do. She decided to seek out the best available treatment and, each day, did what it took to survive. She used the resources around her to support and advise her. And most of all, she did not only have a positive attitude, she lived that attitude. This is not to imply that all a cancer victim has to do is think positive and be committed to survive. Many have such an approach to their disease and fight the good fight but do not survive. They may not survive, but they never fail. To people like Moira, by committing to what they are passionate about, they never fail.

Successful people have found their meaning to life in the goals to which they are committed. They find strength and energy in the challenge and joy of what they are passionate about. Their passion is the fuel that makes them go. They will go to great lengths to pursue their passion and let nothing stop them. Their passion defines them and gives them meaning. Their commitment to their passion is their life.

Is It in the CARDS?

I opened this inquiry with the question, "What is it about successful people or about what they have done that led to their achieving success?" I have discovered that there are five factors leading to success, which are hidden in the cards.

When those five factors are skillfully utilized in playing the cards you were dealt, success will follow. The five hidden factors are the following:

All successful people have a *scheme*.
All successful people know how to make good *decisions*.
All successful people know how to use available *resources*.
All successful people maintain a positive *attitude*.
All successful people define their lives by their *commitment*.

Scheme
Decisions
Resources
Attitude
Commitment

Or

Commitment
Attitude
Resources
Decisions
Scheme

Or

CARDS

The secret to what it is that makes people successful really is hidden in the CARDS, and it is how you play those cards that determine your success.

Journeys to Success

The Declaration of Independence has as its fundamental principle that "all men are created equal, that they are endowed by their Creator with certain unalienable rights, that among these are life, liberty and the pursuit of happiness." While the Declaration of Independence and later the United States Constitution may attempt to guarantee equal rights under the law, it does not imply that all men are equal in their talents, opportunities, and definition of happiness. The human race is a diverse entity with individual differences and a variety of challenges. Skills, obstacles, and supports collide throughout the lives of people, making for an unlimited array of experiences and outcomes. The only thing that is constant is that life is a journey that everyone will take. The roads taken, the mountains climbed, and lessons learned are different for each person.

The stories that follow are of everyday people from a wide range of backgrounds who faced different challenges with a variety of supports but with one common denominator; they were all successful. They are all capable of saying "This is my life, and I did it." Being able to find the self-satisfaction which comes from being happy with oneself may in fact be more important than what was accomplished. These stories are not about becoming famous, but rather, about learning how to play the cards dealt in the best possible way. Such people are more than famous ... they are special. As you read their stories, you will see not only what they accomplished but, hopefully, you will also see how they succeeded. You will see how their *commitment* to someone or something gave them direction and purpose. You will come to respect the *attitude* that fueled their motivation to succeed. You will recognize the *resources* that contributed to their advancing. You will be able to identify the *decisions* they made that were growth producing. You will see the *scheme* that was their journey to success. Yet most importantly, I hope you will come to see in their stories and come to accept in your heart that success is an outcome that is possible for everyone, no matter the journey taken in your pursuit of happiness.

> *The U.S. Constitution doesn't guarantee happiness,*
> *only the pursuit of happiness.*
> *You have to catch up with it yourself.*
> —*Benjamin Franklin*

Jack Ensch
Naval Aviator

As Lt. John C. "Jack" Ensch lay alone on the cement floor of a dark and dingy building somewhere in North Vietnam, his fears for his future mixed with the searing pain he felt in his arms and left hand. He didn't know how long he had been lying there . . . was it minutes or was it days? All he knew was that periodically, he would be yanked up in a chair and be bombarded with questions, only to be thrown back on the ground and left alone when all he would respond was name, rank, serial number, and date of birth. He knew he needed medical care immediately.

Jack had been flying his 285th mission over Vietnam as radar intercept officer (RIO) in a Navy F-4 Phantom when the jet was hit by a surface-to-air missile. With the plane badly damaged and the pilot killed, Jack was forced to eject at over five hundred miles per hour. The force of the ejection ripped off his helmet and dislocated his elbows. The thumb on his left hand lay dangling in his palm as he parachuted down. With the enemy guns firing at him, he parachuted into a rice patty where he struggled to the surface to avoid drowning. He remembered the Viet Cong dragging him out but little else about his trip to this state of pain, silence, and interrogation.

As time passed, he felt himself starting to hallucinate and struggled to stay conscious. He thought about his wife and three small girls and how they would worry. He knew he was alive, but they would not. He thought of how he was a long way from those carefree childhood days of growing up in Illinois. He reflected upon swimming in the rock quarry and playing sandlot baseball all summer with friends. Jack's father worked in a factory as a lathe operator, and while a good provider, Jack's family was not rich materially. It was rich emotionally. He felt the love of his parents and three siblings. He had experienced structure and support in the Catholic schools he attended.

And now he drew on that love and education in prayer and faith. He now kept reminding himself that "God wouldn't give me more than I could endure." Yet the reality of the pain and the draining of his life force started to raise doubts as to if he would make it. Would the Viet Cong just let him die, or would they kill him as they had been threatening? Jack had doubts about his future before—but not life and death.

After high school, he had no direction. He had been a B to C student who others accused of never fully applying himself. So after high school, he drifted into the army where he became a Nike I guided missile system expert. The Viet Cong missile that had shot him down was the exact "stolen" copy of the one he had been trained to fire at enemy planes. The irony of this was not lost to Jack as he lay shaking. While in the army, he was persuaded by a friend to wrestle on the base wrestling team. Upon completing his three years in the army, his wrestling prowess opened the door to his being invited to attend Illinois State University. Life was clear then. He met his future wife and planned to teach English and wrestling upon graduation. But one day, in his senior year, those navy recruiters changed all that and started him down the runway to Vietnam.

More interrogation and threats to his life interrupted his thoughts, but not the pain. He demanded medical treatment, citing the Geneva Convention rule of war. The Viet Cong just laughed at him and called him a war criminal, an "air pirate." Jack Ensch is a war criminal? Jack knew he was no criminal. He was a patriot who was fighting for his country. He was a veteran pilot of four combat deployments and had completed over 285 combat missions. He had been credited with two confirmed MIG-17 kills. He had always been aware of the danger of his career, but had learned to push it back in his mind and find comfort from the training and experience he had received. Yet no training he had received in being a POW was enough to prepare him for this. His arms were discoloring and turning black, and his left hand, wrapped in blood-soaked rags, had become numb. It had been three days since he had been shot down, and his life was fading along with his mind. Then on the third day, Jack's captors decided he would be a compliant prisoner and took him for medical care. They straightened his arms and cut off his left thumb. Jack took heart—maybe he would make it. But the Viet Cong's idea of postsurgical medical care was throwing him into dark solitary confinement for the next month. With no sense of day or night or time passing, with no sound except the threats of his captors, Jack once again retreated into a world of mental discipline to maintain his sanity. He would practice retrieving from memory sonnets he had learned in college and do calculations in his head. And for strength, he would think of his family and pray. While doubts would drift by, his resolve to get home only grew stronger.

After a month, he was released from solitary confinement and joined the other prisoners in the Hanoi POW camp they called the Hanoi Hilton. Even though he was the worst off medically, with the help and mere presence of the other prisoners, Jack knew he would make it home. In fact, he felt at home in the structure and discipline that the POWs had created for themselves. Everyone had their duties and supported one another with a positive attitude and humor. Bolstered by the sound of the B-52s overhead bombing Hanoi in December 1972, the POWs knew that the end of their captivity was near. For Jack, it ended on March 29, 1973, when he was returned with the last group of repatriated officers.

Surviving such an ordeal would be accomplishment enough to fill a lifetime for most people, yet the love of being a naval aviator and the desire to be part of something greater than himself drove him further. Upon returning to the Balboa Naval Hospital, he was told that he would never fly again due to the loss of his thumb. Jack was determined to prove that he could handle the intricacies of being a radar intercept officer without a thumb. He pushed himself through nine months of rehabilitation therapy, determined to earn his wings back. His discipline and dedication once again paid off with his proving to the navy that he could do his job even without his left thumb. As a result, he was not only reinstated as a naval aviator, but was eventually assigned as executive officer of the Navy Fighter Weapons School (TOPGUN).

From there, his career would grow and include numerous positions of leadership culminating as commander of the Naval Training Center in San Diego. By the time he had retired form the navy, Captain Ensch had completed a master's degree in systems management form the University of Southern California and had graduated from the Industrial College of the Armed Forces in Washington. He had accumulated over three thousand flight hours and over eight hundred carrier landings in F-4 Phantom and F-14 Tomcat fighters. He had been awarded the Navy Cross, Legion of Merit (three awards), Bronze Star with Combat V (two awards), Purple Heart (two awards), Meritorious Service medal (three awards), Air Medal (eighteen awards), Navy Commendation Medal with Combat "V" (three awards), Prisoner of War Medal, Combat Action Ribbon, and various other commendations.

In reflecting upon his time in captivity, he speaks of how the Viet Cong never could understand the American spirit. How they could break a prisoner down through beatings one day only to encounter new resistance the next. Captain Jack Ensch personifies that spirit, a spirit that can adapt to changing circumstances while staying constant in his faith and purpose. A spirit that spurns a personal philosophy of "Take what you do seriously, but don't take yourself too seriously." A spirit that is driven by his stated purpose in life: "to continue to grow, to continue to learn, and to continue to contribute." Captain Jack Ensch will tell you that he is not any more special than the next man and that what he has accomplished is no more special than what others have accomplished. But what cannot be denied is the very special "American spirit" that is the man.

Valerie Vigoda
Child Prodigy

In a small club, a spotlight widens on a dark stage, and flashing musical sounds that are a cross between pop and jazz fill the club. In the spotlight stands a confident and engaging athletic-looking blond female, whose dancing fingers and slashing bow work intricately weaves a lively tapestry of notes and melody from her electric violin. The crowd is mesmerized by the complexity of her skill, the energy of her music, and the enthusiasm of her person. Through the course of the evening, the complexity of the music she plays is balanced by the purity of her singing. While physically striking and extremely talented, this young lady blends in well with two equally talented performers as they complement and showcase one another's talents. Their performance is music with a dash of humor, a sprinkle of theatrics, stirred with electricity and baked in their own creative way. The trio is called GrooveLily, and the violinist is Valerie Vigoda.

As I sit captivated and entertained by the twists and turns of her performance, I am even more intrigued in the light of her brief biography in the program. She was a classically trained musician who graduated with honors from Princeton University. It was not surprising, given the talent I was witnessing, that she had toured the world with Cyndi Lauper, been the opening act for Tina Turner and Cher, as well as toured with Joe Jackson and the Trans-Siberian Orchestra. It made perfect sense that she has recorded four CDs of her music to date. What jumped as the dissonant note of her biography was that she was a former lieutenant in the United States Army. If these are the major destinations of her career, I couldn't help but wonder, what was the journey like leading up to the performance unfolding before me?

Valerie is an only child of parents whom she described as "incredibly loving and supportive." Learning and playing music were promoted at an early age, and it was "kind of assumed I would do well." And doing "well" is what she did. By age five, she was reading, and by age eleven, she had skipped three grades and was a freshman in high school. For her, learning came easy, just as music came naturally. Valerie's father is, as she describes, "the greatest jazz pianist in the world." He played in clubs around the Washington, D.C., area and performed with such artists as Quincy Jones and Sting. At home, he would constantly make music with his daughter, inspiring her to expand her talent. At an early age, Valerie was labeled a child prodigy.

As she entered high school, the label of child prodigy became a burden rather than a blessing. Rather than practicing four hours a day, she just wanted to be with her friends. This put a strain on her family. Her parents became fearful about their young daughter spending time with peers three years her elder. They tried to limit her activities, which only made her pull away more. Her obsession to belong socially was so important that it became difficult for her to focus on her studies. She would hide her grades from her peers and purposely misuse a word to appear as one of the crowd. Being taller, confident, and socially outgoing, she had no difficulty making friends. Yet she hated when some boy she was attracted to would learn how old she really was. Such comments as "You would be a cheap date. I would only have to pay for a child's ticket" resulted in her dating very little in high school. By the time she entered Princeton University, she felt she wanted nothing to do with her parents and "I just wanted to feel I belonged."

The same struggles she felt in high school continued in college, and after her freshman year, she took a year off from school. When she returned the following year, she was seventeen years old and closer to the age of a college student. The tension at home reduced, yet she still wanted to be more independent of her parents. Her solution was to join the army ROTC program at Princeton in order to pay for college herself. This was when a transition began. She started to jog, and the once chubby girl with one leg three quarters of an inch shorter than the other started to learn that she was no longer limited to the academic world. "I learned that I could rise to new challenges that I was not used to doing." In the army, she was still being told what to do and how to achieve, yet it was not about her being a child prodigy, it was more about character and taking a risk. "I used to be considered a very special and smart person with a lot of potential, but with each passing year, you are less of a prodigy and more of a normal person. I realized that whatever excellence you want to get out of your life has to come from your own self. I was proud of my reputation but I didn't have to do anything to earn it—I did in the military."

After college, she admitted to floundering career-wise because "I had always been on someone else's track." Her parents, school, or the army had always told her what to do and what was success. After a few years of various musical odd jobs, including being the first sound designer at the Children's Television Workshop (*Sesame Street*), Valerie finished her first album and put together a band. She was now pursuing her music her way, with only herself to push or direct her. She has found that days on the road can be both "wonderful and trying." Performing means seeing exotic places and being pampered as part of a big name tour, as well as experiencing total exhaustion from one-night engagements in small halls where the sound system doesn't work. All the time testing herself and expanding her skills. "I throw myself into situations where I had to improvise." The criticisms of her performance are always outweighed by the rush that comes from pursuing creative excellence. "I could not stop doing this now. Being stagnant is so debilitating to my feeling of being alive." Combining the talent of her father along with the feisty "doesn't care what others think" attitude of her mother, Valerie continues to expose herself to opportunities and challenges while seeing the only true risk in life is one day regretting that "I hadn't tried as hard as I could."

Today, as Valerie experiments with combining the music of a concert tour with the story telling of theater, a song she performs entitled "Are We There Yet?" best describes her.

In a song that Valerie wrote and performs along with Brendan Milburn entitled "Live Through This (Are We There Yet?)" they write:

> But if we can live through this
> We will come out into sunshine
> If we can live through this
> We will be of one heart and one mind
> If we can live through this
> Maybe we'll get the cosmic punch line
> If we can live through this
>
> Are we there yet? Are we there yet?

If the "cosmic punch line" is that success is not a place but rather a process—a process in which you pursue your heart's commitment to its fullest in your own

unique way—then yes, Valerie, you are there now.

Mike Douglass
Fitness Expert

Number 53, the outside linebacker of the Green Bay Packers, reads the formation as the opposition's offense comes to the line of scrimmage. His eyes shift to the guards to steal the first clue of where the play is going. The ball is hiked. The guards pull to lead the sweep away from his side. With lightning quick instincts and speed, the linebacker slices his way down the line, avoiding the wash of blockers, ripping underneath the center who tries to block him. Knowing the tendency of the running back to cut back up field in such situations, the linebacker quickly fills the hole that has emerged and drills the runner backward for no gain. The resulting crash echoes throughout the stadium until it is drowned by the gasp and then roar of the crowd. The great defensive play not only arouses the crowd, it ignites his teammates.

"Ya, Mad Dog!"

"You hurt him, Dog. You hurt the—!"

"You're the man, we got them now!

It is on such a play that the fortunes of the game can turn. From the darkness of apparent defeat, a ray of hope for victory can shine through. Yet for this linebacker, victory had come long before this game was played. It didn't come from a stadium of cheering fans, but rather, on the streets of a Los Angeles ghetto called Watts. For Mike Douglass, his road to victory had more formidable obstacles than that of a furious NFL lineman.

For most fourteen-year-olds, the future is filled with hopes, dreams, and anticipation of freedom. But this is was not the case for a black male growing up in the riot-torn streets of Watts in the late 1960s. For such children, all they could see in their future was being trapped forever in a prison of drugs, booze, and frustration. This was not the life that Mike wanted. He had seen enough adults wasted on drugs and peers shot dead in the streets to know that he wanted to get away from Watts and pursue a future without limits. "No one had dreams in my neighborhood. Their biggest goal was to go to Bob's University, which was the liquor store in the neighborhood where all of the superstars hung out." Once great athletes in high school, they now hung out and got drunk or loaded. Winners on the field became losers in life. "I knew that was one university I did not want to attend."

Mike was the third of five siblings raised by his single mother. His father left when Mike was three years old, taking his oldest brother with him to California. His mother and the rest of his siblings came to California and stayed to fight for custody of his brother. His mother would work two jobs to support the family and provided more than a roof for Mike. "My mother was a strong believer that you could achieve anything if you set your mind to it." She was a strict disciplinarian whose rules and structure made a young Michael come to appreciate the importance of being a disciplined person who sets and achieves goals. His mother also instilled the importance of balance in his life, and Michael realized if he was to get away from Watts, he would have to create as many options for himself as possible. As a result, he never missed school, was an A student, played in the school band, and was a three-sport athlete. "My mom only went to two of my high school games, but she knew what report card I brought home, the paintings I did, and who I brought home. Now my mom talks about the people I influence, not my tackles." From his varied and busy high school schedule, Mike learned that "You set a goal to get to one point then you have to reassess who you are and your values and create new goals to strengthen yourself. If there are road blocks, most people change their goals or give up. I take the challenge to work harder." With the help of caring teachers, for whom it was more than a job, and the love and guidance of his mother, Mike survived the pressures of high school and went off to college expecting nothing would be tougher.

Mike had earned both academic and athletic scholarships and decided to attend Arizona State University. He quickly realized that there was quite a difference between the streets of Watts and the desert campus in Arizona, so he transferred to San Diego State University where he would flourish. Mike excelled both in the classroom and on the football field. In the two seasons, he played for the San Diego State Aztecs, they posted 10-1 records, and he made 193 tackles and 32 sacks. He set the single season record for sacks at San Diego State with 21 in 1978. He earned the nickname of "Mad Dog" from his teammates for his tenacious and aggressive play and the nation's sports writers All-American honors. In 1978, he was the fifth round draft choice of the Green Bay Packers. His talent was about to take him further away from Watts.

The pro scouts had always told him that he would be too small to play in the NFL, so he changed his goals, thinking it wasn't an option. Besides, he had only played football as a means to get to college. He hadn't even seen a professional football game, and now he found himself in the training camp of the Green Bay Packers. As he looked around the camp, he was impressed by the size and the speed of everyone. The other linebackers stood 6'4" and weighed in at 245 pounds or more. Mike was not intimidated because he believed "It's not the size of the man it's the fight in the man. I felt I had more fight than them." He would use his speed, determination, and intellect to become a better player than the prototype linebacker. Yet he knew it would take more than talent to be a great ball player. It would take mental discipline and an ability to analyze the situation. He decided to study more than others so he would know in advance where the opponent's play would be and then use his speed to get there. "I learned to be a good student and applied it to football." But this was still not enough to satisfy the coaching staff. They still wanted him to gain weight. At a mere six feet and 205 pounds, Mike was told that he would have to "bulk up"; translation: take steroids. He felt like he was back in high school. The challenge was no different. Take drugs to fit in. "I said NO! Steriods to me is a drug, and I would never compromise myself to do it." He could see what it was doing to his teammates. They "just reminded me of the people I was trying to get away from." The club required him to weigh in regularly as part of his contract. On weigh-in days, he would conceal ankle or wrist weights in his shorts so the scale would read 220. They would give him the thumbs up and a wink of approval, assuming he was now taking steroids. The truth was that Mike weighed 205 and, by the end of the season, would actually be down to weighing 197. After weighing in, Mike would go back to his locker, remove the weights, and go out to practice. Despite his low weight, in the eight years as the starting outside linebacker of the Packers, he never missed a game due to injuries. He led the Packers in tackles for three years and is second in club history for the most tackles (146) in a single season. He was named as an all-pro four times and was inducted into the Green Bay Packers Hall of Fame in 2003. Before retiring from football, Mike played a season in his new hometown of San Diego.

When we retire from a career, we may leave what we did but not who we are. Mike Douglass could not retire from being the disciplined, tenacious goal setter that had become his trademark. He had become an icon to others in Watts as an example of what it takes to get out and make more out of life. He would frequently go back over the years and tell kids, "I was a product of this environment and by staying disciplined, having goals, and staying focused, I got out." He always thought he would become a teacher but discovered a passion for nutrition and physical fitness. He easily retained what he was studying and became a nutritional expert. Developing his intellect was not enough for Mike. The competitive drive was still very strong, so he turned to body building—natural, drug-free body building. Since 1986, he has won more than twenty-five natural body building championships, including the California State Natural Body Building Championship for five years in a row. "I compete in body building, I teach aerobics, I teach cooking classes, everything it takes to help my client convert to a fitness lifestyle." In addition to providing personal training, writing articles for newspapers and TV, and creating new low-fat recipes, Mike has started a program called "Say No To Drugs and Yes To Fitness" for high school and middle school children.

Mike has come a long way from those dark days in Watts. He is happily married, has a wonderful daughter, and a passion for his profession. "My mother made it clear that I would not fail. It was not an option. I knew I would never end up at Bob's University or on drugs. I just knew I'm going to do it. I never see failure. I just take another approach. The option to fail is not there, the option to succeed is always there . . . you just have to dig deep enough to find it. Your personal goal and your personal success is the only thing that's out there . . . that is your true option."

Anna Laszlo
Social Advocate

For a five-year-old girl living on a vineyard in Hungary with her mother and father, life consisted of running in sun-drenched fields and playing school in her father's classroom. Her father taught physics and math at the university in Budapest and was the headmaster at the small three-room school. Life to young Anna was angelic and filled with beauty and wonderment. She was not aware of the world of her father and of those around who were feeling the repression of Russian occupation. Her father, Frank, had been a first lieutenant with the Hungarian army when he and four thousand other soldiers in the summer of 1945 were illegally seized by the Russians and transported back as prisoners to work in Russia. The harsh winters and limited food resulted in many dying. After two years of enduring, Frank was released. Returning to Hungary, he got married and started the life that Anna had come to know. Yet behind the smiling faces of friends and family that Anna saw were rumblings of discontent over the occupation of the Russians. In October 1956, those feelings of discontent exploded into a movement to force the Russians out of Hungary. Frank became the commander of his town's national guard and aided in forcing the Russian's retreat. As member of the National Freedom Committee, Frank exposed the communists in Hungary loyal to the Russians and gave voice to the cry for reform. But the Russian withdrawal would not last, and the Freedom Fighters soon found themselves overrun. Frank returned home to find a warning on his door that the communist secret police were searching for him. When all public transportation was cut off, Frank knew it was time to take his wife and daughter and flee, leaving behind all they owned and knew. Leaving behind the sunny days chasing butterflies through the vineyards, the cozy warmth of the kitchen, the hugs of friends and relatives—the only world Anna had ever known.

It was a November night when Anna's mother came to her and said they must leave. Feeling confusion for the first time in her life, Anna was told she could choose only one toy to take with her as she and her parents rushed from their home. Hiding in a wagon filled with hay, her mother told her that she had to be very quiet as they lumbered along for hours. The wagon finally stopped, and a tired and scared Anna stepped out to see the river Ardeu bathed in moonlight. The bridge over the river between Hungary and Austria had already been bombed by the Russians. Anna could hear the distant sounds of gunfire and mortar blasts from a nearby town. The men had cut down trees and built a primitive bridge to get the refugees to freedom in Austria. "Anna," her father directed, "climb on my back and hold on . . . and don't look down." Across the logs, they crawled, with her mother behind them carrying the single suitcase with all that was left of their possessions. Once on the other side, someone suddenly grabbed Anna, pulling her off her father's back. She could see her parents being separated and rushed off into the darkness. A terrified Anna was put on a bus with other crying children having no idea what was happening. She only knew that in one short night, she had lost her parents, her home, and the only life she had known.

Anna and the other children were taken to a farm in Austria. Feeling alone and terrified among strangers, Anna feared she would never see her parents again. After what seemed like an eternity, but was really about thirty-six hours, her parents came walking through the door. Her family had been separated as a means of protecting them. There was the fear that the Russians had minded the riverbanks, raising concern of having entire families destroyed if they were on the same bus. Now back in her parents' arms, Anna knew she would be safe, and her world would soon once again make sense.

The Laszlo family went on to Munich Germany in mid-December and stayed in a friend's house while they decided where to go next. One afternoon, in an effort to bring some civility and normalcy to her daughter's world, Eva Laszlo took Anna to a café for some tea and a small cake. Anna smiled as they stepped into the café. It was as if she and her mother were once again at the little village café back home. It didn't matter that they were dressed in the only clothes they owned; today, Anna felt like a princess, not a refugee. Yet as she sat in the café, she could not ignore the men in uniforms at a nearby table. Anna was afraid. Men in uniforms had always meant evil to her, and she had been taught to never talk to them. She tried not to look at them, but she could not keep her eyes off one man who had very dark skin. She had seen gypsies before, but never had she seen anyone so dark. The man, noticing the child's stares, stood up and came toward her. Anna started to cry and hid behind her mother. The man apologized and returned to his table. Shortly after, a waiter came to the table carrying a giant basket of oranges, apples, and chocolates and put it before

Anna and her mother. "I did not order this. I could never afford such a thing . . . please take it away," Eva said. The waiter responded, "It is for the little girl. It is from the American soldier." As they looked up from their basket of treasures, Eva and Anna could not see the man. He was gone. They looked outside for him, wanting to thank him for his generosity, but he was nowhere in sight. It was then that young Anna would learn a lesson that would shape the course of her life forever. As her mother sat with tears in her eyes, she explained to her daughter what a kind and generous act this was. "This should teach you," she said, "that you should never be afraid of people because they look different. Just because their skin is a different color, or their hair is a different color, or their eyes are different doesn't mean they are bad people." She went on to caution her daughter about judging someone negatively for being different or for looking like someone they once feared when in truth "they may be good people, good human beings."

On Christmas Eve, Anna and her parents arrived in America. They expected to meet up with her father's half brother but learned that he had moved to Paris. Sitting in a refugee camp, not able to speak the language and having no money, the family pondered their future. Eva remembered that she had relatives who came to America after the First World War. So after some research, she contacted her cousins in Cleveland, Ohio. With the support of their relatives, they were able to save money and get their own apartment in the Hungarian section of Cleveland. Since Frank spoke no English, teaching was not an option, so he got a job repairing meters for the Consolidated Natural Gas Company. He worked hard not only at his job, but also at learning English and eventually moved up to the position of company controller. Frank had learned that through hard work, he could be successful in America. He was determined to give his young daughter the best education available, which is what he did. Through Anna's love of learning and Frank's drive to financially provide for her, Anna attended Beaumont School for Girls, an exclusive girls' school. Anna went on to earn a scholarship to John Carroll University in Cleveland and then another scholarship to Boston College for her graduate work. Building on the love of politics that ran through her family, Anna was on the road to getting a degree in political science. Yet it was another lesson from her past that would guide her ultimate destiny.

Upon arriving at Boston College, Anna was to work as a graduate assistant as part of her scholarship. Due to a lack of available positions in the political science department, she was referred to assist a professor of nursing, Dr. Ann Burgess. Dr. Burgess was studying the impact of sexual abuse on victims of a crime. She wanted Anna to sit with the victims as they went to court to help them understand the process and give them support. Understanding the legal system was easy for the political science major, but working with traumatized people made her feel lost and inadequate. With Dr. Burgess's help, Anna found that she could relate to what they were feeling. She had felt loss and knew what it felt like having the support of understanding, generous people. Anna started to see that careers are formed when your own skills and past experiences meet up with the needs of those around you. And so was it with Anna who would go on to direct the first Victim Assistance Program in Massachusetts. From there, she would go on to direct and design the development of programs to improve the support for victims of family violence, HIV/AIDS, substance abuse, and school violence.

Anna Laszlo's passion in life is to develop programs to improve the lives of people in need. It is to find ways to provide acts of kindness and generosity to the victims of the world, just as she had felt from that unknown American soldier in a Munich café. Events may change the course of one's life, but it is the lesson learned that determines the direction of that life. Anna has learned that through compassion for your fellow man, you can ease their fear and pain while showing them they are not alone.

Gil Kerlikowske
Police Chief

In Seattle, a beautiful spring Sunday was fading into night when the chief of police Gil Kerlikowske received a call at his home about a homicide. Rarely did the chief of police receive calls about homicides, but this case was different. As the communications dispatcher on the other end of the line put it, "This one is pretty odd." A young well-liked high school tennis coach was found dead in his car along the side of the road, having been shot by an unknown assailant. There were no witnesses, no apparent motive, and no solid leads. When Chief Kerlikowske arrived on the scene, he could see the professionals that make up his department calmly and methodically processing the crime scene. He had confidence in his detectives and crime scene investigators that they would track down the killer, but a sense of urgency kept gnawing at him. His detectives tried to reassure him, "Don't worry, we'll solve it." However, their comments did not make the chief any less anxious. His thirty-four plus years of experience as a police officer was telling him that they needed to do more, and right away. A good person, a husband, and a father of an eighteen-month-old girl was dead. Yet why was nothing taken? It was a senseless crime that could have been committed by a sniper. Such a possibility could terrorize a community and send it into panic. Like a basketball coach seeking instant results, Chief Kerlikowske decided to call for a full-court press that would increase their chances of finding the killer while at the same time demonstrating to the community that they would be kept safe. He called for up to one hundred more officers to seal off the surrounding community, to go door-to-door, to deploy a harbor patrol boat to cruise the shoreline. All night and into the next day, they kept up the search. About noon the next day, officers investigated an abandoned barge where they found a sixteen-year-old male. While interviewing the teenager, one of the officers spotted some blood-soaked clothes in the corner. Clothes that would prove to be the teen's and soaked with the blood of the slain high school coach.

They had found their killer. The young man whom the police had found had faked he was sick on the side of the road. The Good Samaritan made a U-turn and pulled over to see if the teen needed help. When the unsuspecting driver rolled down his window, the teen raised a shotgun and killed him. The case was solved, and a city could relax, but the chief's job was not yet complete. The victim had left behind a young wife and an eighteen-month-old daughter. The victim's wife, and the family who had come from out-of-state, wanted to see the location where her beloved husband had died. The chief stayed with her the rest of the day, walking her through how and where it happened. He knew he could not take away her pain, but at least she wouldn't experience it alone.

A crime seen through the eyes of a police chief is very different and has many more nuances than as seen by anyone else in his police force. The detective sees it as a murder to solve. The CSI look at the crime scene as a wealth of hidden clues. A watch commander sees each crime as a juggling act between calls needing police response while keeping an eye on expenses. The mental health counselors see the needs of the victim and their family as they try to cope with the shock. But a chief of police sees all of this and more. The chief sees the whole picture, which includes how a crime will affect a community with all its expectations and fears. The chief must instinctually know how to balance the resources at his disposal in such a way as to meet the community's expectations and relieve its fears. Such insight comes from a lifetime of experiences that molds a chief of police into a unique and multitalented individual. One such individual is Gil Kerlikowske.

Gil was eleven years old when he and his mother moved from Michigan to Florida to join his father who was in search of a new career. Gil's father was a very talented, handsome, and congenial man who once had a goal of becoming a pharmacist. After returning from military service, he kicked around between jobs, eventually driving a laundry truck in Florida. He hadn't reached his goal to be a pharmacist or even get ahead in life due to his addiction to alcohol and gambling. Gil and his mother came to realize that when it was payday, they had to find him quickly or else he would drink or gamble his paycheck away. Gil remembers at age thirteen going into the Chicken Coop Bar on U.S. 41 filled with hardcore drinkers and saying to his father, "Dad you have to come home."

For as unreliable as his father was, his mother was the opposite. She was always there for Gil. She got a job working in a courthouse for a judge in the small town of Fort Myers. Her place of work was close to their home, and Gil would walk over and spend hours at the courthouse. The policemen who were waiting for documents to be signed would happily sit and talk with the young boy. Policemen became his role models, but so did the judges. A while after his mother divorced his father, she married the judge of the town. He was the self-disciplined, compassionate man that Gil's father was not. Gil looked up to him for who he was as a person and for what he could teach him. In his early teens on weekends, Gil worked at the county jail fingerprinting and photographing the prisoners that had come in the night before. As time went on, Gil was asked to do more around the courthouse and, before long, found himself processing crime scenes and testifying in open court as an expert witness. Not only was Gil's stepfather the city's county court and juvenile court judge, he was also its coroner. By the time Gil was a senior in high school, he was accompanying his stepfather to the local funeral homes, where among stacks of bodies, they would observe the physicians conducting autopsies. Gil remembers being asked by his peers if he was going to go the dance and his replying, "No, I'm going to an autopsy."

Gil enjoyed high school for its fun activities but found he had to work hard to earn Bs and Cs. School was not as interesting as police work! Upon graduating, he left for the "big city" of St. Petersburg and worked part-time as an intern in the auto theft unit of the police department while attending junior college. The war in Vietnam and the impending draft prompted Gil to enlist in the army. After graduating at the top of his military police class, he was assigned to the White House of Richard M. Nixon to protect his helicopter. For the next two years, he traveled around the country protecting the president and his helicopter. Upon leaving the military, he got married, went back to college, and officially started on his journey as a police officer in the St. Petersburg Police Department. That journey would take him to a variety of assignments, from being on an inner-city policing team to being a detective in narcotics, robbery, and homicide. It would lead to his being promoted to the rank of lieutenant and more assignments in Internal Affairs, Vice, and Narcotics and the field training of new recruits. He would become the commanding officer of the Criminal Investigation Division of the St. Petersburg Police Department before he started on his career as police chief. Gil distinguished himself wherever he was assigned, but it is not his impressive resume that best describes the making of the man, it is what he did and experienced in those positions that best tell the story of the making of a chief of police.

In the thirty-four years of being a police officer, Gil, like most officers, has never fired his gun, but that's not to say he hasn't faced life-threatening situations. Once, while working as a narcotics detective, he was part of a cover unit for two undercover officers who were attempting a $25,000 drug buy. Suddenly they lost visual and microphone contact with the officers. Everyone spread out in an attempt to locate them. Gil and his partner returned to where they last had contact with their comrades. As they approached an old house, they heard over their radio the voice of one of the officers pleading for his life. "Please don't shoot me, don't shoot me." While Gil's partner went to the back of the house, Gil entered through the front with his gun drawn. There Gil heard the assailant preparing to shoot his partners. "Drop your gun," Gil commanded, but before he could fire, he found himself in a struggle on the floor, fighting for control of the assailant's gun. He was able to eventually overpower his combatant and make the arrest. Such incidents are not on résumé's but are seared on a policeman's brain as a marker of what is true fear. Gil admits to having been robbed more than once while looking at the muzzle of a gun, facing the prospect of dying. He remembers being as scared as any victim he had helped. A feeling he would never forget when working with victims of a crime.

Not all of Gil's experiences were life threatening, but as a detective, many taught him to see the whole picture and not just settle for what is on the surface. Once a family reported that their sweet, innocent teenage daughter had been kidnapped. A widespread search ensued, and weeks passed before she was spotted in Texas. What actually happened was that she had run off with some hippies to see the country and was unharmed. The only damage was to her parent's previously held vision of their daughter as being responsible and a virgin. Then there was the older woman who had been assaulted when someone forced their way into her house, stole her valuables, and left her unconscious on the floor. She was positive that it was two black males that attacked her. While a search was started for two nondescript black males, Gil did further investigation. It wasn't long before the results of investigation led to the arrest of a white teenager who lived a block away and who had regularly mowed the victim's lawn. That day, Gil admits that he learned a valuable lesson. Not only should a police officer question the possible fallacy of an eyewitness account, but forever be aware of the tremendous power of the officer to influence the interpretation of a case.

Such experiences shaped Gil and prepared him for his journey as a police chief. He was the police chief in Port St. Lucie and later in Fort Pierce, Florida, before accepting the position of police commissioner in Buffalo, New York. There, he restructured the police force into the community policing approach with miniprecincts, resulting in a significant decline in crime rates and an increase in officer morale and community safety. His success led to a position as Deputy Director, U.S. Department of Justice, in charge of the Office of Community Oriented Policing Services, which entailed responsibility for $6 billion in federal investments. While Gil enjoyed this responsibility, he also longed to go back and be closer to direct policing; so after two years with the Department of Justice, he accepted the challenge of being the police chief of Seattle, Washington.

The tenure of a police chief is usually only three and a half years because of the difficulty of satisfying everyone. The chief represents the city officials, the police officers, and the public. You are expected to do more with less. The officers expect you to support them, but you are also responsible to the city and the community. You have to make decisions that are best for the community, which often does not make both sides happy. This is the atmosphere in which Chief Kerlikowske now found himself. Within the first year on the job, the department was accused of racial profiling and was attacked for not directing his officers to be more forceful during the Mardi Gras riots. His officers were critical of his leadership, claiming he was more of a politician than a policeman, and they blamed the low department morale on him. If his first year was not shook up enough, he was then hit with the Nisqually earthquake, which literally shook fear into the community. Gil has never thought he would fail, and he had the self-confidence that he would succeed in Seattle as he had everywhere else. As he says to students, "You shouldn't think that a roadblock or a detour or where you are stalled is the decisive factor that you are not going to succeed. Sure it may take me longer and be harder but it's not a career ender. You just have to work harder." And work harder is what the chief has done. His typical day might include meetings with watch commanders, reading a story to a Head Start class, riding with the gang unit officers, meeting with community leaders and groups, going to the lab to see the progress on a case, and withstanding the personal humiliation for the sake of charity of playing the role of a policeman in the professional musical theater production of *Singing in the Rain* (for which he admitted he would rather had been shot with a taser gun). Through a calm, confident, and steady approach, Chief Kerlikowske has won over his police force and community one person at a time. He still gets his share of criticism and second-guesses from those around him, but today, they see him differently. Through his response to the challenges of his job, Seattle's chief of police is now seen as a well-respected and trusted man who will give an honest answer and even admit when he is wrong. Such dedication, openness, and sincerity are the foundations of leadership.

It is clear that Gil Kerlikowske's entire life has been a journey that shaped him into a chief of police. Yet it is more than a past that keeps him wanting to be a policeman. It is the loyalty to his fellow officers and commitment to protecting his community that drives him to work each day. It is standing next to a fellow officer under fire and an officer's widow at his burial. It is long hours of looking for clues and listening to complaints. It is the smile on a child's face and the look of relief in a mother's eyes. Each day he confronts challenges that he does not want to face, but he does because as Gil has said, "that is what a policeman does." Policemen are role models and the protectors of our society. Leading the way is the local face of the policeman, the chief of police, whose primary job is to instill in the community the belief that they are safe. Gil Kerlikowske is that face, and because of him, the residents of Seattle know they are safe under his watch to pursue their own journey to success.

Mary Catherine Swanson
Teacher

A teacher affects eternity; he can never tell where his influence stops.
—Henry Brooks Adams

One Christmas Eve night, a woman is putting the finishing touches on the next day's festivities while she half listens to the Christmas mass from the Vatican on the TV. Suddenly she hears a familiar name. It is the name of Jaime Escobedo, the same name of a student she taught many years before. Her Jamie was one of eight boys whose parents, having no more than a fifth-grade education, had immigrated to the United States so that their sons could get an education. None of the family spoke any English when they arrived, yet all eight boys received college degrees. Jaime was introverted and had the most difficulty learning English. He had come to his former teacher after entering college to get her advice about pursuing priesthood. As the teacher listened closer to the mass, it was explained that there would be three young priests from around the world assisting the pope that night. One of the priests, joined by his entire family for the mass, was Jaime Escobedo from San Diego. At that moment, the teacher knew that she was seeing the flowering of a seed she had help plant many years ago. Tears came to her eyes and a smile was on her lips as she thought of Jaime and his family's journey. And pride, the pride that is felt by every teacher when they see one of their students fulfill their destiny. But this was not a new feeling for Mary Catherine Swanson, who has, as she walked through the garden of her career, witnessed the flowering of many destinies that came from seeds that were never expected to bloom.

Mary Catherine came from a very educated family. Her grandfather was a college president, and her father, a newspaper publisher. Her mother also came from well-educated roots but was unable to attend college due to the Depression, yet she had completed many courses in business. Growing up in the small central California town of Kingsburg, Mary Catherine was sheltered from such things as restaurants, theaters, and big city issues. All activities centered around the high school, and everyone got involved. She learned that you don't have to be good at everything; just try, and you will improve. She learned the value of hard work, being employed packing peaches at the local cannery by the age of twelve. In her family, doing well was a value. Her grandmother would say, "You will do this and do it well because you are a Jacobs." Despite the family pride the pressure Mary Catherine felt to succeed was internal and not externally induced. She loved spending hours intellectually sparing with her father and being challenged to think.

Her college career started at the University of the Pacific for a year and a half and then she transferred to the University of San Francisco to pursue a degree in English and journalism. San Francisco was much different from the small town of Kingsburg and the sheltered world of the University of Pacific. It was the time when universities and the city were engulfed in the protest movement. There would be police in riot gear on campus, and she would come to class only to learn that her professor was in jail for antiwar protesting. Mary Catherine wrote editorials against civil unrest and was fired from the Methodist newspaper for expressing her conservative views. Despite the criticism she received, she felt it was important to be "part of the debate and be a thinking human being." She had been raised to stand up for her beliefs while also be willing to change.

Upon graduating from the University of San Francisco, Mary Catherine got a scholarship to study journalism at Columbia University. Her dream was to be the next Barbara Walters and travel the world bringing the news to television. But her father had other ideas. Enlisting the help of the chairman of the journalism department at her college, they confronted her with "You had your dream, it is now time to do what women do"—which meant be an English teacher. Since she respected both men, and she really didn't want to move away from her eventual husband, she agreed with their advice and with "no regrets," started to complete her teaching degree. She got her credentials, got married, and started teaching in 1966. After her husband returned from Vietnam, he got a job in San Diego, and she started teaching English at Clairemont High School. She loved teaching, especially the repartee with students and the intellectual discussions. She taught remedial classes initially and found a joy in seeing them improve in reading by two years in a semester. Yet there were changes coming to Clairemont that would change the course of her life forever.

In 1978, there was a federal judge who ordered the busing of students to integrate the schools in San Diego. Since a new high school had recently been built, resulting in a declining enrollment at Clairemont, it became clear that students from the minority sections of San Diego would be coming to Clairemont. Out of fear of the problems these students would bring with them, such as gang activity and lowering of standards, hundreds of the most affluent students and many teachers left the school. Mary Catherine wanted to stay and understand more about the students the school would be getting, so she visited their junior highs and was surprised by what she found. The kids looked bright and had tons of energy but avoided going to class. The teachers spoke negatively about their students and the curriculum due to district mandates consisted of rigid district-wide worksheets. The students had more books and materials available to them than the students at Clairemont, yet something was missing. What was missing was expectation, challenge, and support. These students needed a new approach that would convince them that they could reach goals that they had previously believed was out of their reach, such as going college and living a life that they had feared to even dream of having. They needed to be given the opportunity to excel and be taught how to excel. What they needed was Mary Catherine and a program that would eventually be called AVID, Achievement Via Individual Determination.

The goal of AVID was to get the midrange student with unused potential to become motivated and capable to attend college. Mary Catherine needed a carrot for her students and the University of California at San Diego fit the bill perfectly. UCSD was a new school just eleven miles from Clairemont and had the lowest minority admission in the state. She convinced the administration at the college that if she could get her students to meet UC standards for admission that they would guarantee admission. With that approval, she then recruited her former students who attended UCSD to serve as tutors to the new AVID students. She worked with the district to write a grant to pay for the tutors, which was awarded to her, but before she got the money, a district administrator ran off with the money not to be found. Mary Catherine was forced to seek other sources for financial support, which came in the form of a $7,000 grant form the Bank of America to cover three years of tutors. With the help of a fellow teacher and mentor, Jim Grove, Mary Catherine started to design the program. The students had to be put through a rigorous curriculum while being given support. She was able to overcome most of the school administrator's reservations, but her students were all placed in remedial classes, which never would get them to college. So the Sunday before the opening of school, Mary Catherine snuck into the counseling center and changed the classes of her students from remedial to gifted. The first day of school, the classes were overloaded, and they had to open new sections to accommodate the students. With that, the process of AVID began.

Students from a wide range of ethnic and cultural backgrounds attended Clairemont that first year. Many of them didn't speak English, and few had ever felt successful in school. But with hard work and support, they were successful. With millions of dollars from the federal government, the district had started their own program to help the same makeup of students elsewhere in the district. The curriculum was called the Achievement Goals Program or AGP and taught students directly to the test by which they would be evaluated. After four years, the AVID students scored 47 percent higher in language arts and 35 percent higher in math than the AGP students. This became an embarrassment to the district, and Mary Catherine was ordered to shut down AVID. The new principal at her school was not supportive, and she felt no choice but to leave the school and students that she loved. She was devastated. But the despair lasted only two days to when she got a call from the county office of education wanting her to apply what she had learned in educating AVID students to those in the county schools. From there, AVID grew into a $22 million business found in thirty-six states and sixteen countries. Over fifty percent of the students served are from low-income families who in the past would have dropped out and didn't finish their schooling, let alone go to college. And more importantly, Mary Catherine can tell you stories about doctors, lawyers, teachers, and scientists who would not be now serving and improving society if it wasn't for AVID. One such success story is that of Truong-Son Vinh.

At the end of the Vietnam War, there was an influx of refugees to San Diego. Among them was Truong-Son Vinh. Truong had lost his father in the war before immigrating to the United States with his mother and two sisters. While Truong-Son spoke no English when he came to Clairemont, his mind was like a sponge. He got involved with the other students, and he quickly learned English through exposure to it. He graduated with honors from Clairemont and went to UCSD. While coming back to Clairemont to tutor others, Truong-Son graduated from college in three years. He went on to California Institute of Technology where he earned a master's degree. Before he could start his doctorial program, Truong-Son was hired by Rockwell International to work on guidance, navigation, and control for the Space Shuttle. He also developed the computer simulations to support two Space Shuttle launches. Mary Catherine remembers Truong-Son visiting her after the launches to get her advice about leaving the space program. He and some other scientists had designed an antiballistic missile interceptor system, which they wanted to develop privately. Mary Catherine remembers once again sitting before her television during the Desert Storm campaign and watching Truong-Son's system shoot down the missiles Saddam Hussein had launched toward Israel. Eventually Truong-Son, in an effort to achieve a better balance between work and family, earned an MBA in finance and is successfully working in the financial world.

Benjamin Franklin once said:

Genius without education is like silver in the mine.

Mary Catherine Swanson saw silver in the students around her and, like all teachers, dared to bring it to the light of day. She will tell you that it is not by chance that she and her students have been so successful. "To me it's hard work and common sense and if you don't know it, you learn it. It's also about having a dream and if it doesn't work then do it this way, this way, this way and eventually it will work. I think that's what life is all about."

Gregory Thomas
School Safety Specialist

As Greg sat alone in his darkened apartment, his thoughts drifted through all that he had lost and the pain that he had felt. He thought of his divorce and how he missed seeing and playing with his six-year-old son. He thought about his close friend who had just been killed in the line of duty as a police officer. Such a friend would have known what to say to rekindle Greg's flickering spirit. And then there was his career, or lack of it. For eight months, he had been unemployed. He had gone everywhere, willing to do anything so he could support himself and his son. Not being able to contribute to the support of his son was the worse of it all, especially at Christmas. He had come so far and achieved so much in his life, only now to crash so very low. So low, in such darkness, that he could see no light to guide him out. For the first time in his life, he felt himself starting to give up. He started to think of suicide.

Greg had been riding the wave of success through most of his life. He had been raised along with his older and younger sisters by loving parents. His father had worked late at night at RCA Communications as a teletype operator, and although he wanted to spend more time with Greg, it wasn't possible. It was his mother who provided the "stern discipline" and taught a respect for others, which would characterize what Greg would become. Growing up in public housing in Brooklyn, money was not always available, but Greg had what he needed. "I wasn't born with a silver spoon in my mouth, but rather a plastic fork you get in cafeterias." What he needed was the sound advice and direction of his mother. He remembers what his mother always said. "Have something to fall back on ... have a Plan B." That became clearer to a young Greg when early in his senior year of football, he damaged ligaments in his knee and couldn't start the season. It was then that his mantra became "academics first and athletics second."

His mother also taught him to always treat people fairly and with respect. His mother's wisdom first paid off when he was exploring where to go to college. Greg had been hanging out at the recreation center, as did most of the other neighborhood kids. Greg was different, however. He liked to volunteer to help the center's director, Bob Katz. Bob had taken a liking to this respectful and intelligent young man, so one day, he quizzed Greg about his plans for college. Bob offered to put him in touch with a friend of his at the University of Maryland—Eastern Shore. One visit to the campus, and Greg knew it was the place for him. While there, Greg was awarded a full scholarship for track and field. He established three university track records and was a member of two United States track and field teams. After graduating with honors with a bachelor of arts in sociology, Greg had decisions to make about the many options before him. With his talents, the United States Olympic team, graduate school, or a career as a lawyer were all possible. While fame as an Olympic quarter-miler beckoned, it was graduate school that captured his heart. He enrolled in Long Island University to study criminal justice.

Greg had decided on criminal justice as a career because of the influence of his adopted "uncle" George Savoy. Greg admired how George, a New York City Transit policeman, would conduct himself; he was always looking out for those around him. He didn't flaunt his role, but rather kept his job as somewhat of a secret. George would go on to become a homicide detective. Greg and George would spend hours talking shop. Greg followed George into law enforcement, but his goal was not to walk the streets protecting others, but rather, to help people through investigating and changing social policies. Law enforcement administration was where he wanted to be, so as graduation neared, Greg had another career decision to make. Greg had been working with his father at RCA Communications during graduate school. As the company prepared to move, Greg wanted to stay near to his school, so he quit RCA. He was confident that once he graduated, he would have no trouble finding a job. Unfortunately this was not the case. Greg found himself unemployed with no plan B to fall back on. After repeated rejections, he was forced to go place to place, doing a "cold search" in the hope of finding something to kick start his career. One day, he went to the New York City Department of Investigation in the hope of finding a "help wanted" sign. The receptionist said there were no jobs and handed him a brochure. Dejected and feeling some apprehension about his future, Greg stepped on the elevator to leave. As he looked back, he saw a mature man racing to get to the elevator. Greg held the elevator for the man who gratefully thanked him as the doors closed. Not able to get his quest for a job off his mind, Greg asked the man if he knew of any jobs for a man with his education. After briefly talking, the man told Greg to send him his resume, assuring Greg that he knew of a few jobs available.

"So who are you?" Greg asked as the elevator doors opened.

"I am the commissioner on the back of that brochure," replied the man. He then shook Greg's hand, smiled, and walked off the elevator.

This encounter led to a nine-year career in the New York Department of Investigation, Inspector General Division. He investigated corruption within the workforce of New York City Government on all levels and in all capacities, from undercover operation to administration. From there, he went on to serve on the New York City Mayoral Commission to Investigate Alleged Police Corruption (the Mollen Commission), then to the associate director of City University of New York/NYPD Police Cadet Corps, and then to a position as the assistant fire commissioner in charge of a large bureau responsible for public safety education and recruitment. Greg was on top of his career until suddenly, a list of traumatic events began crashing in on him.

Positions such as fire commissioner are often influenced by politics, which was no exception in Greg's case. As political changes took place, Greg suddenly found himself out of work. His confidence that he would quickly find a job soon evaporated as he found himself in the unemployment line, fearing that he would lose his apartment and wondering about his next meal. Because the unemployment program requires its participants to receive job coaching and instruction, Greg found himself in a variety of job training classes. As he sat there, he wondered, "Why am I here?" He had more skills than those people around him. He could teach the class. He was better than all of this. Then Greg felt that God spoke to him. "You think you are perfect, well you're not perfect. Sit down and mingle. Sit down and become one of the many. Maybe you are thinking of yourself as too high." The humbling experience of those daily sessions opened his eyes to look beyond his own condition into the needs of others.

The eight months of going through a divorce, of being unemployed, and the murder of his close friend and police officer who was gunned down during a robbery attempt totaled enough losses and stress to plant thoughts of suicide. But in fact, those thoughts could never take root due to the support he felt. A retired NYPD detective and "senior mentor" encouraged him to use his time productively and suggested that Greg read a lot, especially the Bible. His parents and fiancée provided constant support and food. There was a list of friends beyond what he could imagine that gave him constant encouragement. And then there was his six-year-old son who put the whole meaning of life into perspective. In his last job with the New York City Fire Department as assistant commissioner, Greg and his son had often rode on fire trucks to fires and ate in the firehouses, so he had dreaded having to tell his son that they could no longer do this because he had lost his job. With tears in his eyes, Greg remembers saying, "Tyler, I will not be going to work at the fire department anymore, I lost my job." Tyler then came up to his grieving father, hugged him, and said, "Daddy, you still have a job . . . you are my father." With such support and love, the seeds of suicide cannot take root.

After eight months of sorrow and growth, Greg was offered a position as the executive director of the Office of School Safety and Planning for the New York City Department of Education. It was his job to assure the safety of all of the schools and agencies in the largest school district in the country. He was responsible for designing and implementing programs for schools so that they would be prepared for any situation that might put children and staff at harm. It was his job not only to design plan A, but also a plan B and plan C, for situations from gang violence to subway disasters. He had learned his lesson about being prepared in life and having plans to fall back on.

September 11, 2001, was Election Day in New York, so Greg decided to take the day off and support some of his friends who were running for office. Their plans suddenly changed when Greg saw the image on the television of a plane in flames imbedded into the North Tower of the Twin Towers. "Get dressed," he yelled to his wife, Kim, who was then a sergeant in the NYPD. "We're back on duty." They quickly got dressed, and with sirens blaring, they raced across the Brooklyn Bridge to, first, Kim's precinct and then his office. Seeing both towers in flames as they drove, tears ran down their cheeks as they thought of the friends they had in those buildings. Greg dropped off Kim at her office in police headquarters in lower Manhattan far from the towers and sped off to his office. Upon arriving, there was little he could do but reassure others and pray that the plans that had been designed and taught were now being executed and effective. That day, there were nine schools in the vicinity of the Twin Towers. They would have to be evacuated through the chaos of smoke and debris that now strangled the area around the collapsing Towers. The *untold story*, as Greg calls it, is that all nine schools evacuated safely with no students killed. "I take zero credit for that. It was the leadership and judgment of those principals that saved those children." The staff and students of those schools were so well prepared and had rehearsed what to do in case of a fire, a water main break, or a subway disaster that the students fell in line and followed directions perfectly. The disaster plans were followed, and when needed, the principals used their *common sense*, which the plan had encouraged them to use when faced with the unexpected. When Greg arrived home later that evening, he was saddened that he wasn't able to get to the schools to help, but relieved that the planning and training he had initiated had saved lives.

He then got a call from his wife. "I'm OK and will be home soon." "Why wouldn't you be OK?" Greg asked. What had transpired was that after Greg had dropped off Kim, she was sent to handle crowd control and the reporters down near the Towers. While there, she suddenly heard a rumbling sound as the South Tower started to fall. "Run for your life," someone yelled, and she ran with the plume of smoke and debris charging after her. She quickly jumped into the doorway of a church just as she was engulfed in a blanket of darkness and concrete dust. When Greg saw Kim upon her return home, her dress was torn and caked with soot. It then hit him how close he had come to losing her, as he had lost his thirteen fire department friends and colleagues that perished that day.

Some might say that those who survived on September 11, 2001, were just lucky. Yet there is a saying that suggests otherwise: "Luck is the residue of design." The students and teachers of the nine schools affected that day survived because they were prepared, not just because they were lucky. Kim was lucky to have survived because she had been trained to remain calm and to use her head in a crisis. Having a plan and a backup plan may not stop the unthinkable from occurring, but it will make a person more prepared to adjust to what needs to be done.

Today, Gregory A. Thomas serves as the director of the Program for School Preparedness and Planning in the National Center for Disaster Preparedness at Columbia University's Mailman School of Public Health. He helps schools nationwide to increase their emergency preparedness. He sits on many boards and commissions that have related interests, including the award-winning Hope Program, which helps impoverished New Yorkers find and keep jobs. Greg's thoughts of suicide are but a fading memory of a stressful time in his life. Replacing such thoughts is the drive to find a better plan to keep more people safe, always remembering the lesson his mother taught him so many years ago: the best plan A is the one that also has a plan B.

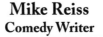

Mike Reiss
Comedy Writer

For over fifteen years, an outrageous, dysfunctional, and, at times, poignant yellow-skinned family has made audiences across the country and around the world laugh. The viewers relate to the comedic actions and words of the characters and laugh because they can draw parallels to their own lives. The combination of creative animators, story tellers, and comedy writers has produced the television icon *The Simpsons*. Each episode is written by teams of writers who bounce off each other's creativity to prune and shape the episode into a collective product. Topics may promote one view one week that is then opposed in the following episode with the only intent being to make the audience and the writers laugh. From the ever-changing brain trusts that comprise the writers have come such memorable quotes from Homer Simpson:

> How is education supposed to make me feel smarter? Besides, every time I learn something new, it pushes some old stuff out of my brain. Remember when I took that home winemaking course, and I forgot how to drive?

> Kids, you tried your best and you failed miserably. The lesson is, never try.

> Weaseling out of things is important to learn. It's what separates us from the animals . . . except the weasel.

> Oh, everything looks bad if you remember it.

One member of the team that has been with *The Simpsons* since its inception is comedy writer Mike Reiss. Mike has won four Emmy Awards for his work as a writer, director, and producer for *The Simpsons*. His television credits include *The Tonight Show with Johnny Carson*, *ALF*, Eddie Murphy's *The PJs*, and *It's Garry Shandling's Show*, where he earned an ACE award for writing and producing. He is also the cocreator of two animated series: *The Critic*, which portrays a lovable movie critic, and *Queer Duck,* the animated adventures of a gay duck. In the world of comedy writers, Mike Reiss could be called famous. "I'm as famous as a TV writer gets, which is not famous at all. I never wanted that. I never wanted to be famous. I'm just so lucky that I got to do things I love to do ... the only thing I know how to do and people like it." In fact, Mike sees himself as just a funny person and writer. He always has been a funny person and writer.

Raised in a loving family along with four siblings, Mike describes himself as being "always just a little different from the other kids at school." Today, laughing at himself, he relates, "It was especially hard growing up because I look so Jewish. I put myself through college modeling for hate literature." He admits that he was a funny-looking geeky kid who did well in school but had an "odd personality." "Kids just liked me because I was funny ... It's just the way I was." He came by his personality naturally, having been born into a family of very funny people. "We studied joke books like other families study the Bible." Comedy had always appealed to him, and by age six, after finding himself being captivated with watching comedians such as Woody Allen, Mike realized that writing comedy was what he wanted to do. "It was something I couldn't help myself from doing. From a kid, I knew this is all I would do." He started writing jokes, comic strips, and comedic stories, which fit right into his family of writers. Growing up, Mike remembers that his youngest sister had put a journal in the bathroom so stories could be written. Routinely, the story would be left for the next family member to continue. Everyone in his family were writers at one time or another. His mother wrote articles for the local newspaper, his sister wrote a joke book, and his father, upon retiring from being a physician, wrote award-winning history books. Growing up, Mike was so passionate about writing that he would dread having to take the time to read a book and write a report. Instead, he would create a fictitious book and write a report on it. His lifelong goal was to become a writer for *The National Lampoon* magazine so he decided to go to Harvard for the opportunity to write for the *Harvard Lampoon*.

Upon graduating from college, Mike achieved his life long goal; he was hired to write for *The National Lampoon*. During its earlier years, *The National Lampoon* was on the cutting edge in the world of satire and had a major cultural influence on its readers. When Mike was hired, the magazine had seen its better days, forcing Mike and his writing partner, Al Jean, to look for other jobs to supplement their income. "At one time, we worked five different side jobs hoping something would pan out." Their first break came when they were hired to write jokes for the movie *Airplane II*. This brought them to Hollywood, where they became part of the network of comedy writers bouncing around from one situation comedy and movie to the next. Through a lot of hard work, "we made our own luck." Mike and Al had been working on the low-rated but critically acclaimed, *It's Garry Shandling's Show* when they were recommended to the producers of a new show called *The Simpsons*. Since when writing for a series, you are on a break for three months out of a year, they decided to take the job offer. Mike remembers, "I thought this was going to be a disaster." It was the first animated series for adults and was to be on the FOX network, which was new and had a poor initial reputation. "At the time, I thought I had hit rock bottom doing *The Simpsons*. It taught me that you should take any job that comes along. You never know what it will turn into."

Mike returns to *The Simpsons* each season as a writer, consultant, director, or producer. His success has allowed him to pursue other interests and creative endeavors. He tried his hand at creating children's books, which has resulted is five such books to date that are both critically and economically successful. He also thought he had a mystery in him, so he wrote a caveman detective story *Cro-Magnon PI*, which won an Edgar Award as the Best First Mystery. It would appear that whatever Mike writes instantly turns to gold, but writing is not as easy as the finished product might suggest. "My writing comes out of long hours of hard work. I think long and hard before a single word is written. I believe in the material, but not before I know I have worked long and hard on it and I think it is good." When he tried to publish his first children's book, it was rejected by a long list of publishers until one took the chance on it. His murder mystery was "rejected by everyone" until it finally sold for $110 to *Alfred Hitchcock Mystery Magazine*, a small magazine with limited circulation. More recently, he wrote a small story entitled the "Fat Man," which was rejected by forty-two magazines. "I couldn't give it away." Believing in what he had written, Mike adapted it to a screenplay, which sold for $675,000.

Mike will be the first to tell you that he has led a charmed life; he was raised in a loving and supportive family, he has a long and happy marriage, and he has the freedom to pursue a career that allows him to do what he loves most—to make people laugh. "I have always taken what I do seriously, but I make sure that I don't take myself too seriously." Even Mike will admit that *The Simpsons* may not last forever, yet this aging program has not lost its creativity and vitality. From Mike's perspective, "Most shows die in their infancy . . . Your average show runs sixty or seventy episodes. *The Simpsons* is a 370-year-old man. We're lucky we can still pee." But what will never decline is the drive in Mike Reiss to write and make people laugh. "That is who I am. That is what I do."

Bill Whittaker
The Coach

On a sun-drenched Saturday afternoon while waiting for my son's freshman baseball game to begin, I noticed that on the field were about thirty or more boys from the St. Augustine Baseball teams congregating in left field. They were players from the school's varsity, junior varsity, and freshman teams in full uniform and arranging themselves for what looked to be a team picture. In the middle of the group was a beardless Santa Claus lookalike, joking and teasing with the boys. He was the only adult in the picture. Out of curiosity, I asked a parent sitting in the stands if he knew what the picture was all about. "That man in the middle is Coach Whittaker," he replied. "He has coached here for years. He has not only coached each of those boys at one time at Saints ... he also coached their fathers." I was to learn later that Bill Whittaker had been coaching for over sixty-five years.

Bill was born and raised in the small cow town of Alliance, Nebraska. At age fourteen, his family needed a change and relocated to San Diego, California. He remembers the total joy of playing with the animals in Nebraska and hanging out with his dad. "My dad was my hero. He could do anything." He had worked as a cowboy and on the railroad before they moved to San Diego where he became a milkman. "My dad was a frustrated athlete." He had gotten a scholarship to play football at the University of Nebraska, but an injury lost him the chance to play, so he went to work instead. The young Bill kept up the family tradition of playing sports. He would play any sport, even if he wasn't good at it. And if there wasn't a game or competition going on, he would create one. During the summer before his eighth-grade year in school, Bill and his friends dug their own high jump pit and filled it with sand. It was while jumping one day that he injured his knee severely enough to need surgery. His mother, whom he describes as the "traditional sweet Irish Mother with a temper," would not agree to surgery because his grandfather had surgery once, and it caused problems with his walking. As a result, of Bill's injury, he couldn't play football that year for his eighth-grade team at Our Lady of Angels. Bill was devastated. Playing sports and football was his life, his passion. One day the principal, Sister Edward Charles, a stern yet compassionate woman who "no one messed around with," called Bill into her office. He thought for sure he must have done something wrong but couldn't think of what it was . . . this time. "William," said the habited commander, "the school's football team doesn't have a coach, and if we can't find one, there will not be a team this year. I want you to coach the team." Since no one said no to Sister Edward Charles, young William accepted his assignment happily. Actually, he was happy about the assignment because it allowed him to be on the field again. "No one on the team questioned me because I was the toughest kid around, and they knew Sister would back me up." Little did Bill know, this assignment was the beginning of a coaching career that would span seven decades.

In 1946, about the time Bill was graduating from St. Augustine High School, he also started working for the San Diego Park and Recreation Department. He would go to school where he played baseball during the day and would work at the local recreation center at night or the weekends. By the time he was a junior in high school, he was running the playground, and during his senior year, he passed the written test to become the senior recreation leader. He remembers that during the summer, he would work eight hours a day, coaching six different teams six days a week. He was credited with starting a very successful parochial sports league that was nonexistent at the time. By the time he got married in 1950, he was making 75¢ an hour, and his career path was set. "You have to have a wife that is understanding," Bill is quick to mention. His wife, Jackie, has had to adjust to the long hours and countless awards banquets, which are the reality of a coach's wife. They are devoted to one another and to their seven children, eighteen grandchildren, and one great-grandchild. Yet during those early years, Jackie admits to approaching a baseball season with its demanding hours feeling as if her husband was in the military and had been deployed somewhere. At times, she felt like a single parent. While frustrated at times, she adjusted to the lifestyle, knowing that what Bill was doing was much more than accumulating wins and losses.

Shortly after graduating from St. Augustine and earning an associate arts degree from San Diego City College, Bill was hired to coach at St. Augustine. He continued to work at the Park and Recreation Department, and his rationale was simple: "I had seven kids. Man, I had to moonlight." During his years of coaching, he has seen the development of many players who went on to play in the major leagues. From the same playground from which Ted Williams emerged, Bill coached Graig Nettle, Bob Gluck, John Watham, Daren Johnson, and many others. "I wish I could say I taught them how to play, but I didn't. They had the God-given talent. I only gave them a love of the game and a respect for it." He gave them something more too. "I just feel you got to have a compassion for people if you are to be truly successful. And maybe to be truly successful that doesn't mean you have to go out and win every game." Bill fondly remembers what Bob Spence, one of his players who would go on to play for the Detroit Tigers and later return to St. Augustine as a teacher, once said a couple years after graduating from Saints. "You know, coach, my dad told me you'll probably be the greatest friend I'll ever have. You know I used to think that if we didn't win some games, it was terrible, but that really wasn't important. The friendship and camaraderie we got was more important than winning a game." That is what it is all about for Bill Whittaker. He cannot tell you how many games his teams have won. But he glows when he tells you about the players that went on to become successful doctors, businessmen, mayors, and coaches. He estimates that nearly fifty of the young boys he coached went on to become coaches.

As I sit in the stands watching my son play, I find myself watching and hearing Bill. "Hey! First baseman, if I had wanted a statue, I would have found one better looking than you." The young first baseman got the message and got more involved in the game. Then while coaching third base, he gave the runner on the first base the sign to steal. When it became clear that the runner did not know the signs, Bill posed on one leg, pointing to second base as if he was a winged Mercury pleading for the player to "steal the base now!" Between the bouts of laughter, I saw the young players respectfully being corrected and instructed if their technique or judgment had been lacking. My son told me years later when talking about Bill that he could be tough. "You didn't want to goof around and make him mad because he would be all over you. But you always knew you could go and talk to him about anything, just like he was my grandfather." It is often said in sports that you want to "leave everything on the field"; in other words, give it your all. Maybe what is most important is what you take from the field ... especially from coaches like Bill Whittaker.

PS. As of 2008, Bill continues to work for the San Diego Park and Recreation Department, supervising and coaching at a city recreation center, as well as coaching the freshman baseball team at St. Augustine. He has the longest tenure of any city employee, sixty-two years and counting.

Caryn Mower
Stunt Artist

On a dark mountain road, with rain pelting down, a car slices its way through the deserted darkness. The driver is distracted, looking for something on the seat next to him when suddenly he looks up, seeing that he is about to hit a woman. Her body rolls over the hood, past the front window, and off the back of the car. The driver stops in shock and panic. Did he kill her? Where did she come from? Is it another tragic accident of a victim who was changing a tire? No, it is an opening sequence in the movie *Identity* staring John Cusack and the woman being propelled over the car is stuntwoman Caryn Mower.

In many ways, this sequence describes many of the truths of being a stuntwoman. The stunt was designed to be a wide-angle shot with the audience seeing the car from the side while the victim hit the hood and flew over the roof on to the cement behind. Caryn knew this would be a difficult stunt, but as usual, she just reviewed what was to be done and focused on doing it. She would admit that many times, she is not clear about what the outcome might be so "I try not to think about it too much . . . just do it." Besides, she would not have agreed to the stunt if she didn't believe she could perform it. She knows that once you agree to do a stunt, you have to do it, or else, you will not work for that stunt coordinator again. Oh, there was no doubt she was scared. "If you don't get scared, that's when you start getting stupid." On the night of the shoot, it was not only raining, but it was also very cold. Ice had formed on the hood of the car, which interfered with Caryn being able to glide over the hood. Instead she would slap onto the hood and be thrown off on to the concrete road . . . with no pads. There were five attempts made to get the shot, and each time, Caryn would get more banged up. That night, while sitting in pain and debriefing the terror of the experience with some friends, she got a phone call. They wanted to shoot the scene again. Her friends told her to say no, but keeping with the code of stunt performers, she showed up the next day. Getting herself mentally up to do the stunt the first time was hard enough, but now, after experiencing the pain five times, she found it harder to go forward. Being a stunt performer is as much of a mental game as it is a physical game. "Mentally you just have to say, OK, it's going to hurt, and just do it." This time, when she hit the front of the car, flew over the roof and off the back on to the pavement, the scene went as it was designed. It was only after she was taking off her wig that she realized that she had split open her head. When the movie came out, Caryn's stunt consisted of two seconds of a body rolling over the car window from the perspective of the car's passengers. The flying over the car and landing on the pavement behind was lost on the cutting room floor. Thus is the reality of being a stunt performer. Many of your greatest feats resulting in the greatest pain are never seen, and your contribution to the movie, only fleeting. Yet Caryn knows what she achieved.

A career as a stuntwoman came naturally for Caryn, being the daughter of two physical education teachers and being a self-described tomboy. "I didn't want to study. I wanted to play sports." Accused of being hyperactive at one time because she had trouble staying focused in school, Caryn contends that she would race through her school work just so she could be free to go play. Despite her parents having divorced when she was young, she felt she had a great childhood. "My parents involved me in a lot of things to allow me to make choices. They supported me to take on challenges." She would play any sport that was around, but especially liked playing soccer. Upon finishing high school, she attended Mt. San Antonio Community College for a year while trying to become a professional skier. When that didn't work out, she started to work multiple jobs, which included being a cocktail waitress at Universal Studios theme park. It was there that she met performers who encouraged her to audition for the part of Red Sonja in the live Conan show at the park. It was perfect for her. She got an opportunity to be physically active through fight and stunt scenes. Once she got the part, she discovered another benefit of the role. "People who watched the show would come up to me and tell me how much they liked the performance. They would want my autograph and their picture taken with me. It made me feel great." She now knew what she wanted to do as a career, be a professional stuntwoman. So with the help of those in the show, she was advised in how to develop her craft and put her in touch with those she needed to meet. She also started the long hours and years of diverse training to prepare herself. Caryn became an excellent fighter in karate, jujitsu, and wrestling. In fact, she even wrestled for a while in the WWF. She became a master in the use of all weapons, as well as a master in rappelling, high-speed driving, and scuba diving. She took acting lessons and mastered stage combat. She also became proficient in the use of "air rams," which spring the stunt actor into the air as if they were being blown up, and the use of "ratchets."

After such training, Caryn started to get some jobs being blown up, thrown off buildings, and crashing cars. "I love it. I can be physical and perform in front of a camera without really being in front of the camera. There is too much standing around as an actress. If it was a part where I could be active, like in a Western, that might be okay." An additional thrill is being able to double for a particular actress, not only for the challenge of the stunt to be performed, but also the responsibility to make the actress look good. While Caryn has had many such parts, being only five feet and five inches tall, she does not mirror most tall leading women. "I get called for the hard jobs. Not half of the women would do what I have done," like falling off balconies, being thrown from speeding cars, and "being trapped in a car, drowning."

Being a stuntwoman has not been without its costs. Despite her success, she still is "hustling" to get parts, which entails taking the initiative to show up at a location where a movie is being shot in the hopes that she fits the vision of the stunt coordinator. Many days she leaves with nothing, only to rush off to the next potential opportunity. "In this business, it is who you know, but once you are in the door, it's your talent that will take you pretty far." While Caryn has gone far, physically the toll has been high on her body. She has had quite a few injuries, including multiple knee injuries, splitting her head open twice, and losing her left index finger. "I don't put myself in dangerous situations, accidents just happen." And then there is the cost to her social life. While she will tell you that she has made excellent and close friends, starting a family has been difficult. "It's Hollywood ... weird schedules, long hours and frequent travel ... if you are not in the business, you just don't understand." So while Caryn would like to start a family someday, she continues to be driven by a passion that she can't get enough of. "I just feel I'm going to run out of time. I try to squeeze everything real quickly into my life without ever having the time to sit back and really enjoy it." But maybe that is the feeling of not only a stuntwoman, but of anyone who is passionate about what they do. Because you can't get enough of it, it all seems to go by so fast.

The next time you watch an action-oriented show such as *Pirates of the Caribbean*, *Buffy the Vampire Slayer*, or *Baywatch*, or if you are in the stands being entertained by the live performance of *Waterworld* at Universal Studios Theme Park, you will see Caryn, yet not see her. She will be the faceless person flying through the air, crashing into buildings, and taking blows from the villain. She will be the one who ignites your adrenaline and stirs your imagination with the creativity, courage, dedication, skill, and passion; that is the life of a stuntwoman.

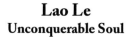

Lao Le
Unconquerable Soul

The sun was hot as the small boat with 280 Vietnamese refugees drifted aimlessly in the South China Sea. Lao sat holding his wife, Kimlien, packed tightly together with the others who, in a quest for freedom, had risked this journey three weeks ago. Now out of food and water, they just drifted to certain death. Lao's thoughts drifted along with the boat to his past and the journey that had brought him to this end.

Lao was the oldest of four boys who were raised in a farming community in rural Vietnam. His parents had stressed the importance of hard work and school, which was not wasted on Lao. He enjoyed learning and, after high school, sought higher education. For a poor farmer's son, such goals were not considered, let alone achieved. But the time was 1968, and many things had changed with the invasion of the Communists from North Vietnam. Determined to defend his country, Lao, against his father's wishes, applied to enter the prestigious Vo Bi Vietnamese Military Academy. To the surprise of many except Lao, he passed the entrance exams and started his training to become a lieutenant in the Vietnamese Army and eventually the elite Special Rangers. He felt proud of fighting for his country. With each battle, Lao's self-confidence grew, and his reputation grew along with it. Due to his courage and leadership, Lao was promoted to captain and given more responsibilities. Then one day, an explosion left him with two fingers on a mangled right hand. A couple of weeks later, while recovering from his wounds in a hospital, the Communists overran the hospital and made Lao a prisoner of war. With his capture, there was no trial, no Geneva Convention rules, not even a record of his existence. For the next eight years, he would work long hard hours, with little food and using only his bare hands as his only tool to clear land and build roads. Guarded in a cell at night, controlled by the Communists, and with no legal rights, Lao drifted with no chance for freedom in sight. As his thoughts returned to the crowded boat upon which he now lay, he smiled as he acknowledged, "I may be trapped and drifting again, but at least I am free."

As Lao looked down at his sleeping wife, he gave thanks that it was because of her love that he now could breathe the air of freedom, even if it was to be short-lived. Lao had met Kimlien in a small park outside of Saigon. Imbedded permanently in his mind was the image of her the first day he saw her. She was a vision of grace and beauty that he was sure must have meant she was an angel. For Kimlien, the handsome, confident officer with the big dreams captivated her thoughts and heart. Kimlien was the daughter of an affluent Vietnam diplomat. It was not acceptable for a woman of such status to marry the son of a lowly peasant farmer, but the love between Lao and Kimlien was stronger than any social barrier, so they married. Their marriage was controlled by the war, which was now raging ever stronger. They found themselves apart often as Lao would be in battle after battle. When he was captured, Kimlien desperately sought any word of him. Once she knew his fate, she constantly worked to find a way to secure his release. But Kimlien was about to have her own challenges and sacrifices that would threaten to trap her in her own prison.

Three years after Lao's capture, Kimlien's family estate was taken over by the Viet Cong, and all of her family's assets were taken. The family found themselves on the streets and needing to escape Vietnam. Her father had wisely buried gold in the backyard, which he used to secure passage to America. As the family prepared to leave, Kimlien knew she could not leave her husband behind. Yet she had her five-year-old daughter, Oanh, to think of. Kimlien thought, *What if something happened to me, what would become of Oanh?* So in a sacrifice of love, Kimlien had her parents take her only daughter to America. As she watched Oanh leave, Kimlien knew that her daughter might be all that would survive as a symbol of the love between her and Lao. Kimlien scratched out survival, selling sugar cane drinks and other food items in street markets, all the while holding out hope for Lao's release. Five years after her family's departure to America, and eight years after Lao's imprisonment, Kimlien, with money from her parents, was able to bribe a communist leader for Lao's release. Since the records would read that Lao had escaped, he and Kimlien decided to race to southwest Vietnam in search of a way to leave the country. There they would find the boat that would take them to freedom.

Ah, this boat to freedom, Lao thought as he watched his fellow passengers smashed together and drifting in and out of consciousness. It had not worked out as he had hoped. Even though the boat was overcrowded, the voyage had started out with great promise. The young Vietnamese naval officer guiding the boat appeared confident that soon they would reach freedom. After four days out to sea, the boat ran aground on a submerged sand barge. Motionless somewhere in the China Sea, the passengers started to panic and lose faith. The captain of the vessel lay ill, unable to function. People's cries and pleas to return to Vietnam rose louder. Lao could not go back. He would not go back. Go back to repression, prison, and probable death. He would rather die at sea, seeking freedom. With passion growing inside him, Lao rose and spoke to his fellow refugees. He spoke of his desire for freedom and commitment to succeed. "Now is the time to do ... or die," he would plead. He then challenged them to follow him into the water to lighten the boat so it might get off the sand barge. He was the first to jump in, followed by Kimlien, and soon the others followed. The boat lifted, and they were able to push it free of the barge's grasp. They boarded the boat and the engine started. Lao was once again a leader, just as he had been on the battlefields. His new troops were not defenders of freedom, but rather, seekers of freedom, and they had faith that he would deliver them safely. Unfortunately, believing and doing are often different things. A day after getting off the sand barge, the engines died for the last time. They now drifted with no way to guide their course. To signal ships for help, the refugees would burn their clothes, hoping to attract a rescue. Ships would pass but not stop. It had now been thirteen days since the engines stopped, and four days since they had run out of all food and water. In the sanctuary of his own mind, Lao wondered if he had made the right decision. Oh, not for himself, for he knew that freedom was his only choice. But what of the others? Kimlien, his angel of beauty who he loved more than life itself, deserved a better fate. If it had not been for her love for him, she would be with their daughter in America, having a future beyond a drifting boat to death. While starvation and dehydration were certain, Lao looked up to see what would cause their eventual demise. A large storm with dark clouds was rising over the horizon. Surely this storm would bring with it the angel of death for all of them. Yet out of the darkening sky came a glowing white ship, and it was coming toward them. It was a cargo ship out of Holland; it was their salvation. The good Samaritans had beaten the storm, and the refugees had beaten death.

The *Neiderkand* provided food and clothing to the travelers and delivered them to a refugee camp in Singapore. The captain of the ship was very impressed with Lao and his leadership abilities. He offered to sponsor Lao and Kimlien if they immigrated to Holland. But Lao graciously refused the offer, desiring instead to be reunited with his daughter in America. Lao and Kimlien spent nine months in the refugee camp before they were processed to immigrate to America. By the time they arrived in San Diego, they had only the clothes on their backs and no money in their pockets. Lao didn't have the money to make a phone call to tell his relatives that they had arrived. Standing in the depot, contemplating his next move, he was approached by a fellow ex-patriot from Vietnam. The man recognized Lao and was glad to welcome a fellow countryman to America. When he learned of Lao's need, he volunteered to make contact with his family for him, thus starting Lao's and Kimlien's life in the land of freedom.

As Lao looked around in the first weeks after his arrival, he knew he was in the land of freedom, but he didn't feel very free. Rather, he felt trapped in worry and self-doubt. On the outside, he would always smile and give the impression of confidence, yet on the inside, he was tormented with the questions, "How I get car?" "How I get job?" "What I qualified to do?" "How can I do this?" Hiding his doubts, Lao started to learn English through the adult school. Whatever the teacher said, he would write it down and study it at home. When Lao enrolled into Southwestern Community College, he found he had no trouble learning physics, chemistry, and mathematics. He studied computers and found he did well, but learning English was very difficult for him. While attending Southwestern, Lao was approached by a teacher who had been a helicopter pilot in Vietnam. The teacher had remembered the captain with the big smile, and the two found a bond that only comes from surviving a war together. Due to Lao's success in school, his new friend was able to sponsor him to receive a scholarship so he could continue his education. It was a great honor, and Lao was very proud. He loved learning. Now he could go full-time and achieve a degree. But it was Kimlien who brought the dreamer back to earth. She had always supported him going to school. She had taken jobs cleaning houses and any other odd job to help support the family. But she was now worried about their growing family.

Shortly after arriving in America, their second child was born, and now there was another on the way. Lao, Kimlien, and their daughters had shared a house with relatives since their arrival. Each family in the house had one room to call their own. They supported themselves through welfare, which proved not to be enough. As a result, Lao turned down the scholarship offer and went to work as an electrician. He soon found that this would not be enough. Sometimes he would not be paid because he would take cash only so as not to jeopardize the little welfare benefits they received. Lao knew that he would never feel free until he could earn a decent wage for his labor and get off welfare. So it was back to school at night; he went to earn an electrician's license. And when this proved not to be enough, he earned a contractor's license and eventually graduated with a bachelor's degree in engineering from San Diego State University. No matter what obstacle was placed before him, Lao would work and study until he cleared the hurdle.

Today, Lao lives in an immaculate middle-class home with his beloved Kimlien and their two youngest daughters who attend college. Their oldest daughter,

Oanh, is now married and has children of her own. Kimlien works as a nurse, and her siblings have established themselves as hardworking, productive, and successful small business owners in San Diego. And while Lao has built a new life for himself in America, he has not forgotten his obligation to his past. He continues to send financial support to family and friends in Vietnam and is active in the Vietnamese veterans association.

When asked what has contributed to his being so successful, Lao does not hesitate in stating that it is having a belief in God and knowing yourself. "God let you have strong powers. You must believe in God." Then "You have to know your capacity, what you qualify to do. Once you know this, you target it right away. I chose the field that I have the capacity . . . I chose right target. Others do not know how to target what they want to be." Lao attributes the knowledge he gained from school and the experience of being an officer in the army as being the foundation of his self-confidence. "Self confidence in my capacity got me on the way." Another contributing factor to Lao's success—although he may be too humble to state, but in reviewing his life, it is so very clear—is his willingness to never give up. No matter what the obstacle—war, prison, lost at sea, or finding work—Lao plowed through the barriers and kept on going. Nothing could stop his spirit to succeed. Perhaps one could conclude that it was a man like Lao that inspired the British poet William Ernest Henley to write *Invictus*:

> Out of the night that covers me,
> Black as the Pit from pole to pole,
> I thank whatever gods may be
> For my unconquerable soul.
>
> In the fell clutch of circumstance
> I have not winced nor cried aloud.
> Under the bludgeonings of chance
> My head is bloody, but unbowed.
>
> Beyond this place of wrath and tears
> Looms but the Horror of the shade,
> And yet the menace of the years
> Finds, and shall find, me unafraid.
>
> It matters not how strait the gate,
> How charged with punishments the scroll,
> I am the master of my fate:
> I am the captain of my soul.

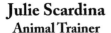

Julie Scardina
Animal Trainer

It's a glistening sun-drenched day at SeaWorld's Shamu Stadium as a capacity crowd oohs and ahs, applauds and squeals with each behavior the shiny black-and-white killer whale performs. Seemingly effortlessly, the giant mammal propels itself out of the crisp fluorescent blue water, gliding through the air, then returning to its natural element, flinging a wave of water over the seated crowd. Almost lost in the blend of the athleticism of the whale, the driving rhythm of the music, and the reaction of the crowd is the trainer, who serves as the quarterback that puts it all in motion. At one point in the show, the whale and trainer swim together in an intricate dance of trust and beauty. Riding on the whale's back, the petite brunette female jumps into the water, assuming a stiff posture that allows the whale to propel her with his rostrum around the pool. Suddenly, both the whale and its seemingly push toy dive deep below the surface and out of sight. The crowd gasps in anticipation. *Where are they? Is she all right?* With the timed crescendo of the music, the whale, still pushing the trainer with his rostrum, thrusts out of the water like a missile going high into the air. Both fly and glide in a coordinated arch back into the water as the announcer cries, "This is Shamu ... and his trainer Julie Scardina."

Just as the Shamu Show is a unique blend of whale and man, so is Julie Scardina a unique blend of a love for animals, intelligence, and perpetual optimism. This blend has led her to being the director of training at SeaWorld, and now the animal ambassador and corporate curator for SeaWorld, Busch Gardens, and Discovery Cove. She makes over a hundred appearances a year, highlighting the park's commitment to animal entertainment, education, and conservation. She has been a regular guest on *The Tonight Show with Jay Leno*, *Jack Hanna's Animal Adventures*, and *The Rosie O'Donnell Show*, as well as appearing on numerous other national TV programs. She also travels the world to promote environmental partnerships to improve local and worldwide conservation efforts. Her career has taken her a long way from the young girl in suburban Chicago who begged her parents for a pet.

From the time she was born, Julie knew what she wanted to do with her life. She wanted to work with animals. Her first word was *horsy*. And as soon as she could read, she fell in love with books like *In the Shadow of Man* by Jane Goodall and other books about the intelligence of animals that would take her to another world: the world of animals. "There never was a time that I didn't feel like I would work with animals." The only problem was how and where to pursue her passion. When her family moved to Southern California, she was eight years old and was able to have more animals around her on a daily basis. As she was finishing high school, she heard of a new program at Moorpark College that taught the student how to care for animals. The number of openings were limited, but she never saw that as a problem, and to her delight, got accepted. It was while being enrolled in this program when she heard of openings for trainers at SeaWorld in San Diego. Again the competition for the position was stiff, and she would have to commute from Moorpark to San Diego, which was over a hundred miles, but this didn't stop her either. Julie was one of the first female trainers that SeaWorld hired, but she never saw it as breaking a gender barrier. She only knew that she was getting a chance to pursue her passion: to be working with animals. That passion would drive her to come in early to work and leave late. She quickly proved her competence and desire, and her gender was never an issue. On her days off, she would continue to pursue her bachelor's degree and eventually earned it from San Diego State University with a major in psychology and minor in biology. The practical application of her degree she was using on a daily basis at SeaWorld.

During her first summer at SeaWorld, she was trained to do the Sea Lion and Otter show. The animals were not very interested that season in performing consistently or even sometimes in being fed. All they wanted to do was to play in the pool. Julie was distraught. A stadium full of people waiting to be entertained, and all that she tried appeared to have no affect on the mischievous sea lion. Putting into practice what she had learned so far at SeaWorld and in school about positive reinforcement and the power of attention, Julie left the stage with the sea lions barking and splashing in the pool. It wasn't long when the barking stopped and the animals started to look around for the trainer they had been tormenting. They climbed out of the water and proceeded to look all around the stage. When they saw that nothing was happening on the stage, they wandered backstage in search of the trainer. It was at that point Julie understood what was the most powerful reward for the animals, attention. She learned that if you give attention for misbehaving, the animal will keep doing it, but if you give attention when they are doing the right things instead, they will work for your attention; but the trainers need to be creative, interesting, and fun. This philosophy of training became the same with all of the animals at SeaWorld, no matter their size or species. Through careful planning and analysis, the goal of the training staff is to create a motivating situation so the animal wants to perform. If this is achieved, Julie notes, "The animal realizes it's a lot more fun and stimulating to do what we are asking of them." So through the use of a variety of rewards from food, to playing with toys, to a loving massage, an atmosphere is developed where they enjoy coming to work. Yet as Julie is quick to point out, each animal has its own personality, and you have to learn about what motivates them at what rate and how they can learn best. For example, Julie has observed that sea lions are much like dogs and like to be active, while dolphins are like little kids with whom you have to be creative about keeping them excited. Killer whales she characterizes as being more like teenagers who have an attitude of "what have you done for me lately?" "You have to work at staying three steps ahead of them and know what they are thinking while still being fun, interesting, and a bit unpredictable."

Julie will tell you that her love of studying and working with animals has always been her defining passion. "There never was a second option." All of her planning was about "what was my next option to get where I wanted to go. If it didn't work out I would have done something different but still with animals." In fact, that did happen for a few years when she felt her philosophies about training and Sea World's were different, and she took a job with the Navy Marine Mammal Program, training sea lions and dolphins to assist the military in combat and rescue operations. No matter where she worked, "As long as I was learning about animals and interacting with them, I was happy." Her pursuit of her passion has also become her philosophy of life. "There have been times when I was disappointed in myself and didn't make the right decisions or questioned myself. But once you make a decision, you have to make it work. You have to deal with whatever comes along and not look at it as something that will prevent you from doing something but rather as an opportunity you hadn't thought of and how can you turn it around into a positive." While you are impressed when talking with her of her passion for her career, what is equally strong is her optimism. Life has not always been easy for Julie, although she doesn't acknowledge that. Her father died when she was young, but she always felt more sadness for her father than feeling sorry for herself. She felt challenged by the long days working and going to school. Even though Julie is very analytical and is grounded in common sense, she openly admits that school wasn't just a breeze for her, and she had to study long hours to earn good grades. But one thing she has always had is a sense that she will always find a way to succeed. She says that life is not a bowl of cherries but rather "Life is like a bowl of Cheerios. You push the Cheerio to the bottom, and it's going to pop right back up to the top. That's the way you have to look at life or your career or whatever. If you're going to get all soggy and stay at the bottom of the bowl, you are right, you are not going to succeed. But you have to work to pop back up to the top because there is a lot of time left after this and you don't know where you are going after this, so pop back up to the top and keep on going and let's see where that takes us." Popping to the top is exactly what Julie Scardina has done—in her career and life.

Bruce Binkowski
Sports Executive

The stadium is filled with excited fans awaiting history to be made as the voice of the public address announcer bellows over the rustling crowd, "Now batting number 8 Bruce Binkowski." It is the final game of the World Series in the bottom of the ninth, trailing by three runs, two outs, and the bases are loaded when Bruce comes to the plate. As Bruce's name is announced, the crowd goes wild, but he hears only a low, muffled roar. His focus is on the pitcher, a formable opponent of Hall of Fame credentials. They greet one another with piercing eyes of respect and determination. Both knew that after this at bat, one of them would be carried off the field victoriously into history and the other would be vanquished in defeat. The umpire yells, "Batter up!" And the confrontation of Titans begins. The pitcher stares in for the sign but shakes off his catcher. Agreeing with the next choice of pitch, he begins his wind up and lets the pitch fly. Bruce gives a mighty swing and drives the ball deep ... deep ... it's going ... it's going ... it's gone! It's a grand slam home run! Binkowski did it; he won the World Series!

Each day, such a fantasy is continuously being played out in the backyards and minds of young boys across the country. Dreaming of winning the World Series with a superhuman performance, they hear the voice of the announcer describing their every move. And they dream that one day it will all come true. One day they will be the hero being carried off the field by an adoring crowd. But the facts are that only one out of every ten thousand athletes who play high school varsity sports will ever play professionally. Due to size, talent, and opportunity, their dreams will fade along with their youth. This was true for Bruce Binkowski. He lacked the size, talent, or opportunity to fulfill his dreams of being a major leaguer, but that didn't lessen his love of the game. By the fourth grade, he knew that as long as he could be part of sports, he would be happy.

Bruce was the third of nine children. His father was in the navy and stationed in Virginia in the first part of Bruce's life. He remembers eating in shifts and sharing bedrooms and bathrooms with his siblings. He also vividly remembers going to his first baseball game with his grandparents, the Philadelphia Phillies versus the Los Angeles Dodgers. He can tell you to this day the names of everyone who played and what they did that day. As a devoted fan of baseball, he would love watching the Game of the Week on Saturdays, mesmerized by the play-by-play calls of Pee Wee Reese and Dizzy Dean. When there wasn't a game, he would read about baseball and collect baseball cards. But now, being at a major league game in person, Bruce felt the world come alive with clarity. He knew he had to be part of this. He had to have a career in sports. He became obsessed with sports. His fourth-grade teacher, Mrs. Lawless, once told his mother, "Bruce is a very nice boy, but he has to learn that there is more in life than sports." For Bruce, sports were *the* only thing in life.

When Bruce was ten years old, his father retired from the navy, and the family moved to San Diego, California. The move allowed Bruce to have his first opportunity to play organized baseball in little league and PONY league. The scrawny kid was aways behind the others on the learning curve, and what skills he had didn't propel him to athletic greatness, but this didn't stop him from playing. To keep the kids off the streets a local coach, Wayne Dorrow had organized the kids at a local playground so they could play every day. And that was just what Bruce did, he played every day, not to become great, but rather for the love of the game. But with high school and the need for financial freedom, the need to focus on the others things in life as, Mrs. Lawless had preached, became a reality. So while going to school, Bruce got a job as a busboy at SeaWorld. His career in sports would have to wait—but not for long.

At SeaWorld, he found himself often working the snack shack next to the Lagoon Show from where he could hear the announcer's baritone voice exclaiming, "Now for the highest jumping bottlenose dolphin in the world. Down she goes and up she comes ... this is Aphrodite!" He could hear the screams of the crowd and feel the excitement the announcer had generated. He started thinking, *I can do that. I can become an announcer.* In fact, Bruce did have a deep mellow voice that lends itself to being an announcer. He had done some announcing of high school basketball games at his high school and liked it even though his peers often made fun of him. So one day, he talked his way into an audition as the dolphin show announcer and got the job. Now he started to study his new trade in earnest. He studied broadcasting at the community college, and when the SeaWorld employees would play basketball games at the local gym, he announced their games into a tape recorder to practice and critic his performance. He started to believe that a career in announcing and sports was possible when he got referred to an internship in the sports department at the local television station. Now opportunities seemed to pop up around him. While going to school, doing his internship, and working at SeaWorld as an announcer, Bruce was offered the job as a statistician and general "gopher" for the minor league hockey team, San Diego Gulls and the National Basketball League San Diego Rockets. He was constantly on the go, but loved every minute of it. He was doing what he always wanted to do; he was in the world of sports. Whatever was asked of him, he did. When they needed an announcer to back up the regular public address announcer, he jumped into the role and *winged it*. Because of his love of baseball, Bruce sought out an interview with Eddie Leishman, the general manager of the San Diego Padres. With his *Baseball Encyclopedia* under his arm, he met with Mr. Leschmen and challenged him to ask of him any question in the book. While the challenge was not taken by Mr. Leishman, he did offer Bruce a job as a runner in the press box during games. Now he was working in three different sports throughout the year.

While his days of working part-time for different organizations were not gone forever, it was interrupted by an offer of a full-time job as a public relations assistant to the Rockets. While he would continue to finish his college degree, this job meant leaving SeaWorld and all the other jobs that he had enjoyed. It was his first office job, and he found that he missed the roar of the crowd and feeling like a star. He started to question if he was in the right place, but once the season started, all doubts faded in the excitement of the games. He felt settled with the Rockets, until one day, he learned a major lesson for those who make a career in sports: nothing is constant. While watching a Padres game one day, he was paged to go to the club president's box. There Buzzie Bavasi greeted him with a smile and a chuckle. "Son, you better call your office. You have been traded." The San Diego Rockets had been sold and would be moving to Houston. So at age twenty-one and never having been away from home, Bruce moved to Houston to continue his duties in public relations. He loved the challenge and the long hours of building something new and exciting. After the first season in Houston, he came back to San Diego to visit his parents and friends. It was on this visit, much to his surprise, that he was offered the job as public relation director of the hockey team San Diego Gulls. It was minor league sports, but he would be the boss and back home, so he took the job. *Ah, I'm home. Time to set down roots*, Bruce thought. But it was not to be. The Gulls folded and went out of business within two years. Bruce got he job as director of public relations for the newly formed American Basketball Association San Diego Conquistadors, but in six months, they followed the Gulls in going out of business. He started to wonder, "I may love sports, but does sports love me?"

Needing to support a family, Bruce took a job in a small local newspaper and prepared for a career as a newspaperman. He had responsibility of a wife and with a child on the way; he could no longer chase a small boy's dream. So Bruce turned down opportunities to go to other teams in other cities for the sake of his family. Yet as he sat alone and reflected, he could feel something was missing. His new career was "nice enough," but it wasn't his passion. It wasn't sports. He missed being part of it—the excitement, the unpredictability, the challenge. Sports was his passion, his reason to go to work.

Bruce would resume his pursuit of his passion when the San Diego Mariners World Hockey Association Team asked him to be their director of public relations. His excitement would last longer than the Mariners, who went out of business six months later. Fortunately, Bruce had learned the lesson of a career in sports and had other part-time jobs to fall back on. One was being the backup public address announcer for the San Diego Padres. As the years passed, his other part-time jobs would include being a radio sports broadcaster on various local stations, being the backup public address announcer for the Padres, and being the director of public relations and first hired employee of the newly formed college football bowl game, the Holiday Bowl. In time, his part-time threads of a career would be woven into an incredible legacy in San Diego.

In 1986, Bruce became the full-time public address announcer for the Padres. He had held the position for years for the San Diego Chargers, but now he was *the voice* of the stadium. When he retired from announcing, if his career had been listed on a sports card, it would read: public address announcer.

- San Diego Chargers—23 years
- San Diego State Aztecs—20 years
- San Diego Padres—14 years ; including 1,101 consecutive games
- Two World Series (1984 and 1998)
- Two Super Bowls (1988 and 1993)
- One All Star Game (1992)
- One Japan Bowl (1993)

While such accomplishments would be a career for most people, it was only part of the journey for Bruce. In fact, Bruce would probably still be announcing if it wasn't for his other "part-time" job. The San Diego Holiday Bowl had grown into one of the premier college bowl games in the country, and Bruce grew with it in his responsibilities. He loved working on a team and organizing a big event. He loved being part of sports. So it was no surprise that when offered the position of executive director of the Holiday

Bowl, he accepted the job. Yet with it came giving up the announcing, which he had loved, because for the first time in his life, he would have to focus on just one job. His evolution in sports was now complete. Everything he had done led to this one position of leadership. He was now the captain of the team. He would be at the center of creating and promoting the Holiday Bowl and all of the other related events throughout the year.

As Bruce looks back at his career, he can see nothing but fun. "Nothing I ever did I considered to be work. It was always fun, my career was my hobby. I have been paid to do something I love to do." While he never played professional baseball, he never felt like a fan either, but rather as a part of the team. He always approached what he did in a businesslike manner, staying focused on his role in the team's success. Only once does he remember when announcing a Padres game did he find himself jumping up and down with uncontrollable excitement. It was when Steve Garvey hit the game-winning homerun after an improbable comeback in the 1984 National League Championship Game, which sent the series into the final game. He remembers quickly recovering and resuming his professional air. But no one would blame Bruce if, while announcing, he would take the opportunity to proudly wonder what those who teased him in high school about his announcing would say now. Or would Mrs. Lawless still think he was "too involved in sports." Today Bruce is often approached by young hopefuls asking what it takes to have a career in sports, and his response is always the same, "Keep plugging away, and if you prove yourself, opportunities will come your way. Don't limit yourself by where you live, and make a commitment to get involved." But above all else, "follow your passion no matter where it takes you." Be it on the field of play or in the announcers' booth.

Mayra Vasquez
Resilience

For the seven-year-old girl with long black hair and big brown eyes, school meant sitting by herself in a corner, coloring or playing alone with toys in the back of the room. Mayra had just entered school for the first time in April because her parents were afraid to enroll her out of a fear that it would be discovered that they were illegal immigrants from Mexico. Because Mayra spoke no English, and her teachers and classmates spoke no Spanish, she was relegated to isolation in the back of the room. She remembers thinking that she didn't like school and would much rather be running free outside or helping her mother clean houses. School only meant being alone and bored. This would be one of the earliest memories of Mayra Vasquez, who would later describe her life as one big roller-coaster ride. For her, the ride had just begun.

Mayra's parents were sensitive to her plight at school, and the next year, they enrolled her in a bilingual school. Here she spent her mornings learning in her native tongue, while in the afternoons, she was required to speak and read English. Here she didn't feel different. Here she could communicate with others and didn't feel so alone. Here she also started to excel in school. By the time she reached the seventh grade and entered a nonbilingual junior high, Mayra was in all advanced placement classes. She was very determined to be the best at whatever she did, be it school or athletics. She would study long hours, and often, she would still be studying when her father would arrive home from work at eleven in the evening. Her father could not help her with her homework because he hadn't attended school and could not read or write, but he would buy her whatever she needed for school. Despite her academic successes at school, Mayra still felt somewhat isolated from her peers and not accepted, so when summer came and she could spend time visiting her aunt and cousins in Tijuana, where she was very happy.

Living with her aunt and walking around the neighborhood, she felt at ease and accepted. On one of her walks with her cousins, she spied a handsome young man sitting in his front yard. At first when she passed, it was a simple nod or a "Hi," but as the days passed, their quick hellos became lengthy conversations, which led to them spending much more time together. Antonio was twenty-two, previously married, and was now living with his mother. Mayra was taken by how calm, quiet, and confident Antonio was; he reminded her of her own father. He also appeared to be very popular because it seemed like he always had friends over to his house, consulting with him and asking his advice. Mayra had never been part of the popular crowd, and now her boyfriend was the most popular of them all. When the summer ended, she returned home and began her ninth-grade school year. Mayra did not want to go back, however. She found herself sneaking back to Tijuana whenever she could to be with Antonio. She always knew where to find him: on the steps of the local church, talking with his friends. Leaving Antonio became harder each time she would return home. One day, she decided not to return home, cutting off all contact with her parents. Her father searched for her everywhere and even hired a private investigator, but could not find his precious daughter. Mayra was determined that her life and future was to be with Antonio: a beautiful life full of beautiful children. Little did she know that the roller coaster was just getting started.

At first, her life with Antonio appeared to be as she had dreamed. He got a job as a tile layer, and each morning after he went off to work, Mayra would clean the house and cook. One day, Mayra walked in on Antonio's mother pleading with him to stop using the needle. As Mayra stood undetected in the hallway, she heard his mother saying something about "leaving that life behind." Antonio only got mad and pushed his mother away. Mayra was confused. She knew nothing of needles and drugs. She had never been exposed to such things, so she just quietly retreated, trying to dismiss what she had observed. She now felt more determined that "this is my life and I will make it work." Yet after about three months of living with Antonio, her suspicions grew. Each day, he would go off to work, and once a week, he would bring her money and his pay stub, but the stub was in his handwriting. Antonio didn't want Mayra to leave the house during the day, yet one day, while fixing dinner, she realized that she needed a tomato. Since the vegetable stand was just down the street, she left home to get what she needed. As she approached the church, she saw Antonio standing with his friends. She thought, *What is he doing there, it's noon?* Suddenly it hit her as if she was in another dimension and as if everything was going downhill. As she approached, Antonio was angry to see her and told her not to come near him and to keep on walking. She would learn later that he did not want her seen with him out of fear that if it was known they were together, that she would be retaliated against. She raced home confused, scared, and feeling alone. That night, when Antonio returned home, he hit her for the first time. Mayra was stunned. She he never seen been exposed to violence before. Her father had been a gentle man who never spanked her or even raised his voice. He was not the stereotypical macho Mexican male, and she had never seen her father and mother even have an argument. Now her world was deteriorating. Antonio now stopped trying to hide his drug usage. His behavior now started to make sense. The quiet calm that she had admired was because he was strung out on heroin. His "friends" were his clients, and his place of business was the place of least suspicion, the steps of the church. Now Antonio would come home often barely able to walk, and the ensuing arguments grew more physical. And as the fighting increased, Mayra's patience ran thin. Soon she found herself exchanging blows. The fights escalated to a daily occurrence, and sticks, rocks, or whatever was close at hand were used to beat one another. Not wanting to be hurt by him or anyone else, she took to sleeping in the roof of the house from where she could see who entered the room below. Most nights, Antonio didn't return home. He no longer brought money home to her, and there was no food in the house. The electricity was cut off, prompting her to use candles in the house for light and to heat water outside to bathe and cook. He sold what possessions she had, leaving her with only one pair of pants and a sweatshirt. While feeling the pangs of hunger, Mayra felt other changes taking place. She was pregnant.

Unfortunately, pregnancy had a zero effect on their relationship; the beatings continued, and on one occasion, he broke her nose. With no money and being anemic, she knew she had to quickly do something to survive. She decided that her salvation would be to find work. She had been raised in a family of hard workers. In the early years, each of her parents had worked more than one job to survive. They would change jobs frequently in the hopes of not being discovered by immigration. Her mother would awake at four thirty each morning to catch a bus to go clean people's houses, and by age eight, Mayra would go and work along side her. By age twelve, because she looked older than her age, she was able to secure a job as a hostess at the Chinese restaurant where her father was a cook. Mayra knew what it meant to work to survive. So Mayra found a job cleaning the house and watching the children of a wealthy family in Tijuana. Each day, she would get the children off to school and return to their house to work all day, repairing the damage they had left behind. For this, she received $2 a day. She used the little money she earned to buy a quart of milk and a loaf of bread, thinking that this would keep her alive and also be best for her unborn child. When she returned home at night, she learned that she had to hide the milk from Antonio or else he would fight her for it. He desired the milk to ease his heroin-ravaged stomach. One day, she couldn't get out of bed to go to work because she was in great pain and had started to bleed. She prayed that she would not lose the baby. While her prayers were answered and she recovered, she had lost a day of work, which meant no food. Prior to this, her parents had discovered where she was and had pleaded with her, through her aunt, to return home, but Mayra refused. She remembers thinking, *I put myself here, and I will get myself out of here on my own.* One day, when about five months pregnant, her father came to her to deliver his plea in person. He wanted Antonio and her to come live with him. Her father was unaware of the Antonio's drug abuse or his abuse of Mayra. He just wanted to help his daughter, and if to do so meant helping Antonio, then so be it. Her father offered to get Antonio a job and to provide whatever they needed. But Mayra refused his offer, citing it was her responsibility to solve it herself. He then gave her an offer she could not refuse. "If not for you," he said "then do it for your baby. It's not his fault." Even Mayra's determination and pride could not argue with such logic, so she and Antonio returned to San Diego to live with her parents. As she stepped into her parent's home, she felt safe again, and her hopes rose that this just might work.

Unfortunately, the upward rise of her roller coaster would be short lived. Antonio refused to work, and he continued to use and sell drugs. Each day, he would leave in the morning, and at night, return in a drugged stupor. One day, when Mayra was in the seventh month of her pregnancy, Antonio did not return home, leaving behind his wallet and all of his possessions. Mayra was frantic to find him. They searched everywhere. For months, she cried, longing for his return, but he would never be seen by her again. She would find out many years later that after he left her, he continued his life of selling and using drugs for many years, until one day, he was killed in a drug deal.

With the birth of her son, Mayra had mixed emotions. She didn't want him out of her sight, yet she could not hold him. It was her father who first held the young one in his arms. She had no drive or strength to do anything at first, but as the months passed, the drive to take care of her son grew strong. She now had a new purpose, a new reason to succeed. Yet she learned that succeeding wasn't that easy. She still seemed to attract men who were losers and addicts. She worked at different jobs to help support her son but had no real direction in her life. It was then that she met a man that would challenge her to return to school. He was a positive role model, and she started to believe that she could take herself to a better place. She felt the return of the fire and determination to learn and excel. On the same day she walked in and passed the test of General Educational Development (GED), she enrolled in community college. She felt almost numb to anything but school, accepting any job that would work around her classes. During breaks in class, she would call home to help her son with his homework, and when she came home, she would study well into the night. By taking classes year round, during the summer, and in between sessions, Mayra was able to graduate with her bachelor's degree in three years. *But what next?* she would think. *Where do I go from here?* It was one of her professors who, seeing Mayra's compassion and love of children, suggested that she pursue her master's degree in school psychology.

Today, Mayra is a school psychologist serving elementary schools in a heavily concentrated Spanish-speaking population. She works with young children who, as she once did, are trying to learn English and to adjust to the roller coaster of life. While her roller-coaster life is an example of the power of determination to succeed, it is also an example of how determination, if misdirected, can nearly destroy you. Determination blinded by denial and pride drives one off course and into a downward spiral. But determination when focused in a positive direction can be the way off the roller coaster and on to a straighter journey to success.

> **David Solove**
> Clown

A circus is a vibrant tapestry of moments weaved together into one unforgettable memory. The crack of the lion tamer's whip, the grace of the flying trapeze artist, the grandeur of a string of elephants raising their trunks in unison are just a few of the vignettes that blend with electrifying music, sizzling colors, aroma of popcorn, and anticipation of the crowd to form the circus experience. In every circus, there is one common thread that is ever present, tying these sensations together and eliciting the defining emotion of a circus; the thread is the clown, and the emotion is joy. Be it throwing pies, falling down, or playing tricks on one another when in the spotlight, or joking with individuals in the crowd or quietly handling rigging in support the acrobats, the clown is everywhere; he is the face of the circus.

There is more to being a clown than face paint, baggy pants, and oversized shoes; you have to have the gift of being a clown. David Solove is a clown with the Ringling Bros. and Barnum & Bailey Circus who has the gift. "To be a successful clown, you have to be true to yourself. Even though I have on a red nose, makeup, and purple hair, I'm me. I have to let myself be who I am. I don't put on a façade. I take what works best for me, which is my people skills and my height [5'3"]. It's a lot easier for me to get down to a child's level than the clown who is five foot eight." For David, being successful is measured by making people laugh. "I love the close interaction with the people. I will go up into the crowd and play with a family and attempt to create such a moment of joy that they will never forget the purple-haired clown that made their family feel special."

David admits that he has been a performer his whole life. The Muppets were and still are his idols, and as a child, he would put on puppet shows in his basement for anyone who would sit still long enough to watch. He knew he wanted a career as a performer after his first appearance on stage as a dancing bear. By high school, he was active in the theater, especially children's theater. He was fortunate enough to be chosen by a lottery to attend a high school that specialized in the theater arts. There, he was popular and accepted, which he thinks might not have been the case at a traditional high school. In his senior year, he wrote a children's play and took it on tour to the local elementary schools. When he enrolled into Syracuse University as a theater major, he continued to perform in children's theater. As he neared graduation, he discovered Ringling Bros. and Barnum Bailey & Circus Clown College. At the time, he was not thinking of becoming a clown but thought the experience would give him skills he could use in children's theater. During his junior year in college, he studied for a semester in London during the centennial celebration for Charlie Chaplin. For the first time, he started to appreciate being a clown as he watched old films of the silent-film star. After two seasons working as a performer at Busch Gardens, David got accepted to the Clown College. As he looked around at the other would-be clowns, he started to get the feeling that he had what it took to be a great clown. Unfortunately, he was not offered a job upon graduation. Despite being disappointed, he wouldn't let such a rejection stop him from pursuing his performing career. He went to auditions and got various parts, always secretly wishing that some day he would be with the circus. He didn't have to wait long. Two months after graduating from Clown College, he got the call. "We need a clown with the blue tour. Report to Cincinnati immediately." And so it began; a boy from Columbus, Ohio, was to start a career in Cincinnati, Ohio, as a clown in "the greatest show on earth."

The life of a clown in the Ringling Bros. & Barnum Bailey Circus is not your run of the mill nine-to-five job. Here, clowns are part of what David refers to as "a city without a zip code." Two trains crisscross the country for eleven months, rolling into more than ninety cities a year. On those trains are three hundred performers in personal quarters the size of a restaurant booth, with animals everywhere. Families travel together with their children being taught by a full-time teacher who travels with the circus. There are long days of parading the elephants at midnight to the arena, setting up the show, rehearsing, making and repairing props, and performing as many as three shows a day. There are the early-morning radio interviews and afternoon TV appearances to publicize the circus being in town. There are the bruises and injuries of a gag gone bad. The area called Clown Alley, where the clowns put on their costumes, is often so cramped that they are stepping on one another. Such togetherness can foster conflicts but also can lead to deep friendships. Having good people skills is a must. The time away from the circus consists of running errands and sightseeing. Being in a town for a week allows little time to develop any long-term relationships, which is particularly rough for a sensitive single person like David. Yet he doesn't complain, but rather, focuses on the deep friendships he has built with the other performers. His is the life of a performer, which means, "When I go through the curtain, any problems I have are lost. When I'm out there, *I am a clown!*"

To pursue such a life, it takes more than greasepaint and a road map. It is not a life that most parents would envision for their child, especially when the child's father is lawyer and his mother is a successful business manager. Yet his parents have always been supportive of David, "allowing me to be me." Such support has encouraged him to take the journey to pursue his passion. David admits that he loves the traveling and friendships attached to a life in the circus, yet what really ignites his soul is the performance, making people laugh. "I love it more now than when I started." A performer has celebrity status. Being a clown is great because I can have the celebrity status but then take off the grease paint and have my privacy. I can walk by a family that I made laugh earlier, and they never recognize me." David has the talent to be a clown, which he feels cannot be taught. He also has the drive to make each performance exciting for his audience because "no matter how many times we have done the show, this is still the audience's first time seeing it." Such concern for detail and dedication eventually led David to becoming the "boss clown," the clown in charge of all of the other clowns and the quality of their performances. He takes pride in knowing that he is part of the illustrious history of clowns in "the greatest show on earth."

David was a clown with Ringling Bros. for eleven years, the last four as boss clown. When he left the circus, he and two close friends and partners started to perform at SeaWorld in Orlando, Florida. Their skits continue to bring smiles to the faces of thousands of the parks visitors each day. Gone is all the travel, yet performing in one place has made possible what was so difficult for David to find on the road, a wife. While the location of his clowning may have changed, the drive to make people laugh continues. It just goes to show you can take the clown out of the circus, but you can't take the circus out of the clown.

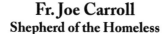

Fr. Joe Carroll
Shepherd of the Homeless

San Diego, California, is known for its pristine beaches, sun-drenched climate, and incomparable zoo. It is the home of unlimited possibilities for the sports and the arts enthusiast. Each year, thousands of tourists flock to its shores to experience what many call paradise. Yet as in many cities, living there is not paradise for everyone. For a large number of people, the city streets and the expansive beaches are their only home. For the homeless, it's not about paradise, but rather, about survival. Fortunately San Diego has an innovative coalition of programs and services that has been endorsed by the Department of Housing and Urban Development as the prototype for a homeless rehabilitation facility. Under the umbrella of Father Joe's Villages, thousands of homeless have been able to better their lives and develop increased self-respect. Based upon a common-sense approach, a continuum of care is available, from being able to take a shower to getting medical care to being trained and placed in a job. While the philosophy for success has been to use common sense in solving the problem, it is clear after seconds of talking with the guiding spark behind the Village that this leader is anything but common. His relaxed, open manner, the twinkle in his eye, and the chuckle in his voice quickly make you feel like you have been friends forever. You feel pulled into his world of acceptance, laughter, and belief that anything is possible. Such a person may use common sense as his credo, but there is something very uncommon about the priest called Father Joe.

Joe Carroll grew up in a family of ten in a two-bedroom apartment in the area of New York City called the Bronx. He and his three brothers would sleep in one bedroom, his four sisters in the other bedroom, and his parents in the living room. His parents were both immigrants from Ireland, who—even though from the same small town in Ireland—had not met until they were in New York. Joe's father never finished elementary school, and his mother never finished high school, yet they both knew what it took to raise a happy family. Joe's father was a laborer, and his mother would clean doctor's offices at night, always being home in time to wake her children up for school. Growing up on the streets of New York in a poor family, Joe quickly learned what it took to get what he wanted. "If I wanted a new pair of shoes, I would play cards to get them. I usually won." What made his youth particularly happy was that he lived around the corner from the Catholic Church. It was there that he became active in sports, the Boy Scouts, and any other activity that the church offered. Due to his personality and being so active in the church, Joe became known as a do-gooder, a reputation that came in handy more than once. "If I got in trouble, the whole neighborhood would blame the other person because they knew I couldn't do wrong." With his siblings, such a reputation had no weight. "If I got home before my brother, I would wear his good shirt on a date and get beat up the next day." In school, Joe was a good student, but especially so in math. On one occasion on the eighth-grade regency exams for math, he missed one question. He wrote a letter protesting that the question was in error due to a comma being in the wrong place. The directors of the test agreed with him, and he kept intact a string of 100 percent performance throughout high school. Math came very easy to him, and he loved it. Over the first weekend of a term, he would read the entire math book and answer the all the homework questions. He would then sell the answers to his classmates throughout the remainder of the term. To this day, he admits he drives his staff nuts because he can look at a budget and instantly spot the errors in the math.

On the day he graduated from high school, Joe moved into his own apartment, which quickly became the primary party time location of all his friends. His apartment had fourteen beds, so if someone was too drunk to go home, they could crash there until they sobered up. The joke around the neighborhood was "Who *didn't* have a key to Joe Carroll's apartment?" He had rules for his guests. There would be no smoking or dirty jokes told in his apartment. A guest would have to go outside if they had to do such things. They were also welcomed to drink the beer or soft drinks in the refrigerator, but there was a price tag on each item that must be paid before consuming. He discovered that since he was also the coach of the softball team, having a local shelter for his friends proved to be much more convenient when it came to waking up hungover ballplayers on Sunday morning. Joe enjoyed his friends and his life, but he did not enjoy the cold winters. Since he suffered from arthritis and had knee surgery when he was eighteen, he found the winters to be particularly unbearable. So one cold winter day, with a postcard of sunny beaches out west in hand, he announced to his family he would be moving. While they laughed at him, it didn't stop him from buying a suitcase from a pawnshop, packing all that he owned in it, and buying a one-way ticket to a place called California.

When the young twenty-year-old landed in California, he had no place to stay, no job, and only $50 in his pocket. He had gone from running a shelter for his friends to being homeless. Joe quickly found someone to move in with and got a job as a checker and bagger in a grocery store in Santa Barbara. He would later work for the post office, but he still had not found a real career direction. One day, he met a priest who quizzed him about his future career plans. Joe responded that he was confused over pursuing a career as a Boy Scout executive or a pure mathematician and, "way down there somewhere," the possibility of being a priest. "That's perfect," said the old priest. "A priest gets to count the collection and be the Boy Scout chaplain, so it solves the problem." At first, Joe fought the idea of becoming a priest. He knew that the old priest was trying to sell him, just like the priests had tried in New York when they would invite him to visit the seminary. For him, visiting the seminary was a chance to get out of the city and go swimming and had nothing to do with becoming a priest. One thing Joe knew about himself, which is true today as well, was that "I don't like being told what to do. Don't tell me I got to do it." Everyone in his neighborhood always said he would become a priest, and he did not want to prove them right. But he finally concluded, "God never leaves you alone until you are happy. He chased me until I entered the seminary." Even after entering, he did not tell his parents where he was for two years to avoid the eventual "I told you so." Joe admits that the old priest had convinced him to enter the seminary, but he was not convinced that this was the career for him. "I was a mediocre seminarian. You needed a 2.5 to graduate, and I had a 2.51. I did just what was necessary to do, nothing more." After four years, he got "kicked out" of school because "they didn't think I had the right attitude for serving God and giving up everything and all that kind of stuff." Since he was something of a wheeler-dealer, "They said I was the kind of priest that would sell gold frames on baptismal certificates and I said if it makes a few bucks, what's the problem?" Joe describes his attitude then as "OK, you badgered me, but I'm not putting my heart into it because I don't really want it. If God's calling me, then great, it's his thing, let him go. Why should I care?" After leaving the seminary, Joe taught for a year and found that he did care. He finally accepted the call and returned to the seminary to complete his studies into the priesthood.

Now that he had decided to complete his training for the priesthood, he looked for a diocese that would take him. The diocese in San Diego was "desperate and would have taken anyone who was alive." So Joe was assigned to the University of San Diego for a year and then was sent to the seminary in Washington, D.C., for additional education. While in Washington, he found living and teaching on campus had its advantages. The faculty was allowed to have televisions and other amenities in their rooms. The only problem was that such items were quite expensive and beyond the reach of many of his colleagues and himself. This didn't stop Joe. He knew that liquor was very expensive in New York but was tax free in Washington, D.C., so he would buy the liquor in Washington and would sell it to his family in New York "at a slight markup." He would then contact his brother-in-law who was a wholesaler in New York and buy televisions and stereos at a 40 percent discount, which he would then sell to the faculty for "a slight markup." He admits that it was a very profitable four years he spent in Washington. At the end of those four years, Joe was ordained, and it was time for Father Joe Carroll to go to work.

Fr. Joe's charm, warmth, and creative energy quickly endeared him to the parishioners of the parishes he was assigned. His success caused him to transfer parishes often before he was ready. On one such occasion, he was transferred to an inner city parish in Southeast San Diego. Fr. Joe protested because he didn't feel he had completed what he had started at his present parish. But the bishop, Leo Maher, knew something about salesmanship himself. "You're good with kids," he told Fr. Joe. "Don't you think inner city kids need youth programs? I just know you can get those kids involved in the church." St. Rita's was situated in the minority section of San Diego and consisted of a large Afro-American and Hispanic population. The church had great facilities but limited participation by the youth of the community. To attract the youth, Fr. Joe offered to take any child in the community to Disneyland for $10. The fee charged certainly didn't cover the expense, but that didn't bother him. He got what he wanted, a list of over five hundred children who would eventually make up his youth group. Others marveled at his success in attracting so many kids, but to him, it was merely common sense. "What kid doesn't want to go to Disneyland? You have to let kids be kids. If you meet them where they are at, they will follow." As his congregation grew, he found himself serving more of another population who frequented the area—the homeless.

One day, Bishop Maher called in Fr. Joe to tell him that he had another assignment for him. He wanted him to lead the project to build homeless shelters. "Why me?" Fr. Joe protested. Staring him straight in the eye, the bishop replied, "Because you, Joe, are the best hustler in the diocese." Once again, Fr. Joe's calling was not of his choosing. He admits that at the time, he would have much preferred remaining where he was working in the parish and thought he might get his wish after the first commercial he made to raise funds. In commercial, he announced that he was a hustler and needed money to help the less fortunate. Rather than sending him back to the parish, his honest plea for help resulted in thousands of dollars in donations pouring in. He was now a celebrity and forced to be a publicity-seeking salesman. "I'm a shy introvert and don't like being in the public eye, but the job demands it. I would much prefer to be in the background, but this job calls for another person. God called me to this job, so you change your personality." There was more than his personality that changed. The treatment of the homeless made a dramatic change, built upon common sense. "It's not hard to figure out what the homeless need, the word defines it. You need a place to live before you can go off to work." As he raised millions in contributions, Fr. Joe built not just shelters, but also a one-stop-shopping approach to rehabilitation. A homeless person now can get a shower, food, housing, job training, and placement, as well as treatment for any physical or mental health problems, all through Fr. Joe's Villages. All along, success for Fr. Joe was measured not by how many people he served became tax-paying citizens, but rather, did the services meet an individual's needs. Needs that have ranged from getting a child into school to providing a transient with clean sheets upon which to die. In the faceless world of the homeless, Fr. Joe worked to give one person at a time an identity, sense of worth, and dignity.

Fr. Joe would probably admit that he wishes he had more control over the path and events in his life. Besides having a lifelong battle with arthritis, he has struggled with diabetes, has endured fourteen knee surgeries, and has had to recover from a stroke. He has heard the piercing criticisms of those who feel his aggressive salesmanship is not befitting a priest and that he is nothing but a two-bit hustler. Yet he has never let such things dictate his life. He does not bemoan the past nor look too far into the future but rather, focuses on getting the most out of today. His heroes growing up were Mickey Mantle and Richard Nixon because no matter what might have knocked them down, they always got up and went on. Like his heroes, Fr. Joe believes, "No matter how often I've lost battles, I still haven't given up and never will." He admits he is not perfect, yet each day strives to "get a little better." A man who could have made millions of dollars for himself believing he is the master of his own fate, finds himself following God's plan for him to raise millions of dollars for the homeless. In Fr. Joe Carroll, God chose a common man, with common sense, to address an all too common problem. He chose a man whose determination to give everything inside him to others led to a very uncommon result.

> But just as you excel in everything—in faith, in speech, in knowledge, in complete earnestness and in your love for us—see that you also excel in this grace of giving.
> —2 Corinthians 8:7

Jeffrey Mitchell
Trauma Responder

In New York, firefighters valiantly struggle to reach two small children in a burning apartment building only to discover their charred bodies. In Florida, after a hurricane, a crisis response worker spends twenty straight hours, hearing one terrifying account after another. In Colorado, paramedics race against time to save a drowning victim but never revive him. In Missouri, an emergency room trauma team frantically tries to stop the bleeding of a young, innocent gunshot victim, but fail. In California, rescue workers feverishly throw cement and debris aside as they race to free a family after an earthquake, only to find them all dead. In Iraq, soldiers search for survivors of a suicide bomber but only find body parts of comrades and children. The images that are left behind from such experiences often haunt and cause deep suffering in the lives of those whose primary purpose was only to relieve suffering. Many times, first responders and those who provide support in a crisis become the additional casualties. This was just what happened to one first responder from whose journey through pain would come a system that today is being used around the world to aid the witnesses of trauma in the process of recovery. The system is called critical incident stress management, and the first responder who created it is Jeffery Mitchell.

Jeff was the youngest of six siblings raised in the small apartment in Brooklyn. While he remembers his family struggling financially, there was never any doubt in his mind that the family was rich in love. His father worked for the YMCA during the days, and his mother worked as a key punch operator in a bank at night. Even though his parents rarely saw each other, they both found time to volunteer in the community—his father as the Boy Scout leader and his mother in church activities. It was from them that Jeff learned the importance of giving to others. In college, he first studied to be a priest but changed his mind after feeling such a career would artificially remove him from people. He considered studying medicine but was poor in math, partially due to having been traumatized by a seventh-grade teacher who got so frustrated with his inability to answer a question on the board that she plunged her pencil into the top of his head. Such an experience may have contributed to his interest in becoming a school counselor or psychologist. Jeff also had developed an interest in firefighting, stemming from his brother being in the New York Fire Department, so while in college, he started to train as a volunteer firefighter. The more he learned, the more he got "the bug." He started to take one class after another. He got certified as a firefighter, then as an ENT, and then as a paramedic, all the time going to school while volunteering in the fire department.

Upon completing two master's degrees, one in counseling and one in clinical psychology, Jeff took a job teaching in an elementary school. He liked teaching, yet when he met Arline Kelly, the direction of his career would change forever. Arline was the director of Maryland Shock and Trauma Center. She took an interest in the twenty-six-year-old volunteer firefighter and elementary teacher and saw potential in him that Jeff hadn't even imagined was there. Arline asked Jeff to become the regional coordinator for the center. His job would be to set up and manage trauma services for a 1,500 square mile area in southern Maryland. He would have to establish the entire emergency response system, including communication, helicopter transport, and coordination of emergency personnel. He would have to decide how to coordinate three hundred ambulances responding in connection to thirteen major hospitals. Jeff admits that he wasn't so sure he was up to the challenge, but Arline felt differently. She saw in Jeff not only talent, but also a drive that would not allow him to give up. Jeff worked long hours overcoming the skepticism of others and his own frustrations. He developed a self-confidence and an attitude that "once you know you are right you are right, hold your position." His drive to succeed led to long hours of work and a focus, which often came at the expense of developing personal relationships. It took some time, but he finally realized that he had to strike a balance between his drive to succeed and a home life. He eventually decided that it was time for him to return to school and complete his goal to get his doctorate in psychology.

By day, Jeff would go to classes, and at night, would work at the local fire department as an ENT. It was one night as he was driving home from the fire station that he came upon a traffic accident that would change his life. A car had run into the back of a pickup truck with long pipes extending from the truck bed. One of the pipes appeared to have rammed through the window of the car on the passenger side. As he approached the car in the darkness, he made out a bright white form in the passenger side. He looked into the car, and there was a young woman in a wedding dress with the pole impaled through her chest. Jeff instinctually reached in to check for a pulse but suddenly felt a blow to his head. "Don't touch her. Get away from her," yelled the victim's drunk groom. Jeff remembers thinking, *He is probably so drunk that he doesn't even know what he has done.* The image of that night, Jeff could not escape. The woman was but a year from his own age. She was supposed to be starting her new life that night; instead, it was the end of her life. Thoughts of her and what he had witnessed would return to his mind daily, being triggered by everyday occurrences, such as the sight of a wedding dress, a similar truck, the sounds of sirens. He knew he needed help but discounted seeking help from doctors or psychologists because he felt they could never understand what he had seen. Only other first responders could relate to the horror that now threatened to consume him. So one day, he told the firefighters at his station what he had been experiencing and asked how were they able to cope with such experiences. To Jeff's surprise, he was told that they all had such images at one time and that his feelings were a normal reaction to the abnormal experiences that they must face. What they had learned that helped control the feelings was to sit around as a group and talk about what they had mutually experienced. By doing this, it seemed to put it to rest.

Jeff found relief talking with his fellow firefighters, but he also found something else. The psychologist side of him translated what he had learned and experienced into the steps of debriefing that could apply to anyone who had experienced a traumatic event. By sitting with those who had a similar experience, the traumatized has a common bond and resulting feeling of acceptance. By clarifying the facts and normalizing their experience, they are allowed to find a new perspective and hope for recovery. And by sharing their feelings in a supportive, nonjudgmental group, they can release what scares them. Firefighters say that before you can put out a fire in a building, you must first ventilate the room to get the smoke out so you can see the source of the fire. Jeff realized that the same was true for the visions that clouded his mind. He had to clear them out so he could heal.

Today, the Critical Incident Stress Management techniques that were designed by Jeff are used in all fifty states and around the world. They are being used in firehouses, police stations, and on military bases to help those in trauma's path to recover. Almost daily, Jeff and the thousands who have been trained in his approach hear comments from victims like, "You helped me through it," "You saved my sanity," "You changed my life." If you were to ask Jeff, he would say, "I have a mission. I have a vision. I know what I am doing is making a difference. And if I died now, I could say, 'I made a valuable contribution.'"

Great contributions to society come in many forms and in many ways. In the case of Jefferey Mitchell, it was a passion to help others along with the training as a first responder and psychologist that was welded together by the lighting strike of a single event that would grow beyond a single individual's personal success.

Kathleen Sellick
Hospital CEO

Kathleen doesn't know why she always wanted to be a candy striper. She just remembers not being able to wait until she turned fourteen so she could volunteer at St. Joseph Hospital in Phoenix. For a shy girl who found making friends difficult, helping the nurses and patients made her feel like she was important and belonged. She remembers vividly the time she entered an elderly patient's room, finding him terrified, confused, and frantically pressing his call button for help because his IV had come out. Kathleen ran to get a nurse to help the man she could not help. She liked being able to help and grew to feel comfortable talking with any patient and walking into any room, except for one. The door of that room was always closed, and behind it was John, a seventeen-year-old boy who had leukemia. Kathleen would see family members come in and out of the room with pained looks on their faces. She felt compassion for John and his family and what they had to go through, living in the hospital. Every time she saw the door, she thought that even before he died, his life had been taken away from him because he had to be behind that closed door. One day, as Kathleen walked upon the unit, the door was open, and the room was empty. John had died, but the memory of that door stayed alive in her heart and would become a symbol of her destiny.

Kathleen grew up in a stable, loving family where Catholic values and the importance of doing your best were stressed. She was taught that "life isn't about you, it is about what you give back." Since her father was a pilot for an airline, she and her family could take monthly trips across the county. It was on these trips that she started to develop a sense of confidence that she could adjust to any situation or place. While she got to travel often, the importance of being frugal with money was obvious in her family. Her mother sewed many of her cloths, and Kathleen started working when she was fourteen years old. She was a good student and became active in a diversity of school activities as a means of making more friends, all the while working as a candy striper at the hospital. It was during her freshman year in college that she returned to St. Joseph's Hospital to speak to the younger candy stripers about what it was like to be in college. It was after her presentation that the chief executive of the hospital, Mr. Huff, approached her with a proposition that would define the course of her life. After talking with her mother, Mr. Huff had concluded that Kathleen would someday make an excellent hospital administrator. He promised her that if she graduated college with a high grade point average that he would see to it that she got into one of the top business schools in the country for graduate school, the University of Chicago. Kathleen had always been attracted to a career in a hospital, but since she was terrible in science, being a doctor or nurse was not an option, so she had decided to major in finance. Now Mr. Huff had given her the way to put her talents toward fulfilling her passion.

After four years of studying, working to raise the money to go to graduate school, and always volunteering at the hospital, Kathleen entered the University of Chicago, Graduate School of Business. It was there that the shy girl felt at home among what she would later refer to as the "nerds like me." She felt like an "intellectual lightweight" compared to her fellow students, but she also felt she was accepted both socially and academically. Upon graduating, she started her journey as a hospital administrator.

By the age of twenty-four, she had become the second highest administrator of a small hospital, and her professional and personal growth had begun. It was then that her secret panic that maybe she would not succeed and that she really didn't know what she was doing started to flood her brain. She would call this the "imposter stage" of her career. Each day she would hope that she wouldn't blow it. But in time, fear gave way to the realization that "you are going to blow it, just fix it." A philosophy emerged that "you are not doing enough if you don't mess up, but then clean it up as quickly as humanly possible and don't do it again." Armed with a developing confidence in herself, Kathleen moved from position to position in the health care industry, realizing that if she had figured out a problem in one setting, she could figure out the new problems in the next location. She learned that you can't be afraid to "go of it," especially as a woman. She had seen the male-dominated world of chief executives and wasn't afraid to point out the inequalities of pay and treatment. After years of being a woman in a male-dominated business, Kathleen's advice to young women is "still be a woman, be your own style. We are not men, yet don't be afraid to show that you are just as smart and strong as them, while being consistent with your feminine side." She also has learned that as a woman, "you can't have it all, and anyone who tells you can isn't telling the truth." Kathleen has a husband and a young daughter, both of whom she loves deeply, but balancing being a perfect mother and the chief executive of a large hospital, she has discovered, isn't possible. She has debated cutting back on her career and being at home more with her child, but she has come to realize that "life is about compromises. If you want to do a job like this, you have to have backup systems, such as your spouse, to make it work. Don't beat yourself up, you can't be everything to everyone, it's not possible. Decide where you are going to put your effort and get the support, knowing you can't do it all."

Today, Kathleen is the chief executive officer of Rady Children's Hospital in San Diego, California. The hospital handles 80 percent of all the medical needs of the children and adolescents in the county, treating 150,000 patients a year. The facility is growing into one of the foremost medical centers for treating children in the country. When asked about the challenges she now faces, she talks of the deep sense of responsibility and obligation she feels to the employees and patients of Children's Hospital and to their families. She is driven to provide for those who work in the hospital what they need professionally and personally so they are better able to help the kids they treat. And for the patients whose lives depend upon Children's, she sees to it that there are no closed doors obstructing their getting the best care possible. The young candy striper has gone from not being able to reach the dying boy behind the closed door to being the chief keeper of the doors, who has dedicated her life to seeing that those doors always stay open.

Frank Patrick
Father

It is morning and another day to commence the routine of getting the kids off to school. While Beth prepares for work, Frank gets Sara and Nick out of bed, fed, and ready for school. Sara, a junior in high school, heads off with her mother to be dropped off on her mother's way to work. Later, Frank walks Nick to his elementary school, chatting about sports, the bug they just saw, or anything that might pass through an eight-year-old boy's mind. When school is over, Frank will pick up the kids and chauffer them, depending upon the time of the year, to their soccer, basketball, baseball, or dance practices or whatever else they might be doing. If there are no practices or games, then there is always homework to be completed under the supportive direction of Frank. This has been the weekday routine in the Patrick household since Frank retired from teaching. His focus is to be there for his kids and give them what they need to grow into healthy adults. Yet there is more growing here than just the kids.

When Frank Patrick is asked what it was like for him growing up, he will say, "I had a great childhood." He will say that because to Frank, everything is great. He remembers fun times with his mother and father, always positive teachers, and neat experiences visiting a neighbor's ranch. But it wasn't all so great. He also remembers the fear he would feel every time his parents would argue and, when seven years old, the confusion he felt the day his father left him and his mother. He loved being with his father and playing catch, talking, and hanging out with him at his work. But all of this stopped, and he would never see him again.

Frank's mother only had an eighth-grade education, and the only job she could find was as a waitress working split shifts at the Santa Maria Inn. This meant that young Frank would be left at home alone for much of his day when not in school. This worried his mother. She had seen what happened to other children in the neighborhood who had limited supervision, and she didn't want this to happen to her son. She loved Frank very much and would sacrifice anything for him, even what little time she had to be with him for the sake of his safety and development. So she found a family who would take in Frank as a foster child on the weekdays and would provide the supervision and direction she knew she could not provide. The family was very nurturing and treated Frank as one of their own. When the parents bought something for their son, they did the same for Frank. They would discipline him when he needed it and praise him when he earned it. On weekends, Frank would be with his mother, and no matter how tired she was, they would do something together that was fun. Frank seemed to know that his mother was doing what was best for him even though she missed him deeply. He knew she worked hard not only to support him, but also to fight her alcoholism. She couldn't hold her liquor, and he had seen her get uncontrollable so quickly. Despite this, he knew she was deeply devoted to him and he to her. While he was embarrassed by her drinking, he would rationalize it away as a by-product of how hard she worked. And he never forgot the lessons she taught him to always remember where you've come from. Even in later life, when Frank was a school principal, she would introduce him as a custodian just to remind him to respect the working man.

Frank's freshman year in high school was a time for change and new directions. The family he was living with had grown, and it was harder for them to house Frank. His mother was still concerned about the issue of supervision when she was gone. She decided that it would be best for Frank to enter the Army and Navy Academy about 150 miles south of where they lived. Frank saw it as another adventure, so why not. It was there that Frank learned some important life lessons about structure, taking orders, and studying. He also learned something else about his untapped talents. He was an excellent football player. Due to some notoriety he had received when he was visiting a peer back home, he was introduced to the head coach of Hancock Junior College who offered him a scholarship to come play for him. Al Baldock was more than a coach; he was a mentor and surrogate father to Frank. He taught him to scuba dive, checked up on him daily, and was an ever-available source of advice and direction. The once B to C student started to excel in the classroom and on the football field, where he was named junior college All-American running back.

Frank always knew if he was going to get to college, he would have to earn a scholarship. His mother had always made it clear that it was not "are you going to college" but rather "which college." Due to athletic and academic skills, he started to get scholarship offers and decided to attend UCLA as a running back. He was full of pride and enthusiasm that first day of practice, picture day. As the players were being placed into formations for the pictures, he got confused. He ran over to the coach and asked, "Where do the running backs go, coach?"

The coach looked at him and, without hesitation, said, "Frank, you're going to be a guard."

Frank played his junior season as a guard, but by the end of the season, he was battling injuries each week. It was in the early weeks of practice his senior year that Frank started to question what he was doing. He was watching a drill called bull in the ring, where one lineman is in the center circled by all the other linemen. When the coach gave the signal, one by one, the linemen in the circle would charge the one in the middle and try to get past him. As the drill progresses, more linemen charge in, until the "bull" is finally overrun. As Frank watched the lineman try to fend off his attackers, he saw the crazed look in his eye and drool flying from his mouth. Frank thought, *That is what I look like. What am I doing here?* That day he walked off the field, never to return. He had to give up his scholarship, find a job to finish college, and start a new adventure.

Without football, new possibilities opened up. After completing his degree, Frank was drawn to theater arts and television broadcasting. One of the classes he took involved him going to an elementary school to film kids for a television program. After completing the filming, the school's principal came up to him and remarked about how well he did with kids and how "he should consider being a teacher." His words echoed in Frank's mind and brought back memories of an eighth-grade teacher he admired who had said the same thing to him many years before. But life for Frank was no longer about what to do, it was what he had to do. It was time to make some money. So he took a job as a claims adjuster. But as the job became more boring to him and less satisfying, the advice to be a teacher came drifting back. Teaching was Frank's passion. To see children grow both academically and emotionally became his purpose in life. He could see that something special was happening, and he was part of it. Frank worked in education for thirty-two years at the elementary and junior high level before retiring. He spent seventeen of those years as a principal, returning to the classroom for the last five years of his career.

Working in education was his passion, but it did not fully complete him as a person. After two failed marriages, something was missing in Frank's life. Yes, he had a wonderful daughter he loved intensely from his first marriage, but she and her mother had moved a few hundred miles away, and Frank could not be there for her as much as he wanted. Frank remained positive, but that is because that is what Frank is, positive; yet he was alone. That changed when he met an energetic, dynamic second-grade teacher named Beth. She had come from a large family and had a loving and nurturing aura that attracted Frank. They soon got married and had Sara and Nick. Frank now felt complete.

The true definition of our place in life is more a reflection of where we've come than where we arrived. And if we are lucky, life sometimes provides us with "do overs" to reconnect the links that were broken in our past. Frank had always missed the connection with a father and the security of a family. While he didn't let what was missing ever dampen his enthusiasm or confidence for what lay ahead, it did leave a feeling of being incomplete, not being whole. Through the love from Beth and the fathering of his children, Frank has been refathering himself. As he does for them, he is experiencing the fathering he never got through them and in so doing, successfully connects the missing links of his past.

> In every conceivable manner, the family is
> link to our past, bridge to our future.
> —Alex Haley

John Box
Manufacturer of Freedom

In everyone's life, there is adversity. Some see adversity as the source of their demise. Others see adversity as the cross they must bear. For a unique few, they see adversity as a blessing, as an opportunity to be successful. One such person is John Box.

John was raised by supportive parents in what he describes as a Christian household in the city of Orange in Southern California. His father worked seventy-hour work weeks in an aerospace company, and his mother was a stay-at-home mom charged with keeping her eye on three very active boys of which John was the youngest. John's father, who spent much of the time out of the house working, still had a major impact on his development. In addition to teaching his sons to stand up for themselves, John's father also taught them that if someone said you couldn't do something, then it was your duty to find out how to do it and do it faster. They were to shoot to be the best and never settle for second. If beaten, their father directed, you were to congratulate your opponent and then work harder to beat them next time. John got the part about standing up for himself, which he did on such a regular basis that he became a frequent visitor to the principal's office. His knack for standing up for himself got him the reputation of being something of a rebel. And the rebel tended to take his own course when it came to school and academics. He was a good student in his early years at school, but sitting in class studying things of little interest to him started to make little sense to him. He excelled in any class that involved using his hands and his mechanical aptitudes. He had been raised in the world of fabricating, and he enjoyed envisioning something and then creating it. By the time he was fourteen, he was working full-time. He enjoyed earning money so much that he dropped out of school. While he enjoyed the world of work, John understood that he still needed a high school diploma, so he went to school at night to complete his education. John felt free, self-sufficient, and in control of his life . . . until one fateful day.

On November 1, 1981, John was riding along with a friend down a beachfront road on their motorcycles. A car that was being driven aggressively suddenly changed lanes, clipping John's bike, sending him flying across the road and under a parked car. His bike then rammed into him at thirty-five miles per hour, causing extensive damage to the trapped fallen rider. As he was carefully pulled from under the car, his rescuers could see that John's foot was injured, but they were more concerned about possible internal injuries. He was rushed to the hospital and straight into surgery. The impact of his cycle hitting him had resulted in a severed aorta, a punctured lung, and a ruptured stomach. The surgeons patched up his aorta and the other damaged organs and sent him to recovery. But he wasn't there long before he had to be raced back to surgery because he was still bleeding internally. John was dying; the surgeon moved quickly and aggressively to save his life. The problem was found, and the bleeding was stopped, but not before some blood came in contact with his spinal cord. In the context of frantically trying to save John's life, blood on the spinal cord seemed inconsequential, but in fact, it would leave John paralyzed for life.

When first told that he would never walk again, John didn't believe what was being said, but as the days passed, the reality of what had happened started to sink in. As he thought more of the prospect of being paralyzed for life, he became more deeply depressed with each passing day. *I'm a vegetable. I'm done*, he found himself thinking. By two months into his recovery, he found himself seriously considering suicide. If he could not experience life with the exhilaration and independence that he was accustomed to, then he would end his life. His doctor, sensing John's struggle, came to his room one day and sat next to his bed. John will never forget the words spoken to him that day. "John," his doctor began, "you may think that you are a vegetable now, but really, you are at the bottom of a mountain. If you think of life as a mountain, you are at the absolute bottom. Some people in life go partway up the mountain. Some go halfway, and some go to the top. You have to decide how far you want to go." His options became clear to him. He could challenge himself and live life or shoot himself. He started to make two lists to help him to decide his fate. The first list had all of the things he would never do again. "I will never walk again; I can't race top fuelsters again; I can't make love, so I won't have children or a girlfriend." On the second list, he had all the things that he could still do and experience in life. As he wrote, he realized that this list was very long. He then asked himself, "Do I want a life without the things on the first list?" His answer was not only that he wanted to live, but rather that he wanted to experience everything that life had to offer. His rebellious attitude returned and, with it, the belief that if someone said he couldn't do something, then he would prove them wrong.

So John's quest to experience life began, not with great victories at first, but rather with small triumphs of human persistence. He remembers sitting and staring at a door, wondering how he would ever be able to open it and get through it. He had to learn how to get in and out of a car, how to navigate a kitchen to cook for himself, and how to get on and off the toilet. One of the things that he wanted to do before the accident was to build a monster truck. The door of the truck he was constructing was well off the ground and a chore to enter even for those with two good legs. There was no way he could use the conventional method that a paralyzed person uses when getting into a car of sliding across from his wheelchair into the seat. He had to climb. With only the use of his arms, he climbed and struggled to reach the driver's seat. As he flopped into the seat, he felt a rush of exhilaration for what he had achieved, but he also felt the reality of a very wet seat. The truck had been left outside, uncovered, and now he found himself sitting in a bucket seat of water. With every victory came the next challenge.

John found that there was very little he couldn't do. He proudly would say, "The only difference between me and you is our mode of transportation." He also found that many of the things that were on his list of lost possibilities in his life was really not as long as he had thought, including getting married. As he recovered further, John went back to work with his brothers in their aerospace business and started to compete in wheelchair tennis tournaments across the country. Successes on the court and his competitive nature drove him to do better with each match. He got ideas of how he could improve his wheelchair and, thus, his chances of winning. One day, he made an appointment with the manufacturer of his wheelchair to share his ideas. Upon arriving at the corporate offices after driving four hours to get there, he was told to come back some other time. They didn't have the time that day to see him; no one had the time for him. As he drove back home, he got mad and swore he would never buy another chair from them. Upon getting home, he met with his brothers, and together they built the wheelchair John had in mind. The chair was considerably better than those of any of his competitors. His fellow athletes regularly asked him to build one for them, but John found himself too busy with his aerospace shop to meet their requests. After a couple of years, he did start to build some wheelchairs for his friends in his spare time. As the requests increased, so did his interest in creating and refining his chairs. The demand for his chairs grew so much that he decided to leave the black-and-white world of an aerospace machinist for the innovative and challenging world of manufacturing wheelchairs. John, along with his brother, not only built their new company into a highly successful business, but John had found something that had become even more important to him. He felt like he was helping others.

While John lay recovering in the hospital, the brash, self-centered teen started to learn the most life-altering lesson of all. While helpless and feeling depressed, he saw nurses, doctors, friends, and strangers being sincerely concerned about him. People he didn't even know were working overtime trying to make his life better. People he didn't even know existed in his church were cheering and praying for him. The compassion that he felt opened his eyes to look beyond himself and see the needs of others. It reshaped his view of the world and his purpose in it. "I wake up each day believing that I'm changing the world in one little way. It may be showing a kid how to do a wheelie in their wheelchair or producing a positive ad campaign. Whatever it is, each day, I try to make life better for someone." While such a philosophy may alter how one looks at life, it doesn't have to change how they pursue life. "My life mission is to challenge, to look for adventure. It will be exciting. It could be negative, but possibly what is negative could become positive. It's just the way you look at things."

Today, John blends his quest to help others with his passion for adventure into his daily life and his company. He actively pursues off-road racing and any other pastime that involves speed, creativity, and a challenge. According to *Fortune* magazine, John has built his business, Colours Wheelchair, into an up-and-coming small business with over $2 million in annual sales. His eye-catching, high-performance wheelchairs with names like Hammer and Spazz are used for everything, from downhill racing to hockey. He and his company have sponsored competitions for disabled athletes across the country, giving participants the chance to feel the exhilaration of challenging themselves through athletics. Yet possibly more important than building wheelchairs is how he markets what he builds. He challenges people with disabilities to see themselves as just as capable and valuable as those with functional legs. He is not hesitant in releasing advertisements with a pregnant woman in a wheelchair or a disabled woman in sexy lingerie. He has started magazines that portray the active and provocative lifestyle that is open to the physically challenged. "I believe that the disabled are no different from the nondisabled, and it is time we end the stigmas attached to the disabled." Through his company and its advertising and products, John hopes to "sell self-esteem" and instill an attitude that there are no limits. For his portrayal and the advancement of people with disabilities, John has received a Media Access Award and the Harold Russell Award.

For John, recognition from others is not what his life is about. He will tell you that the greatest thing that ever happened to him was the accident that left him paralyzed. He will tell you how it increased his social awareness and taught him what is really important in life. It taught him what it takes to meet challenges and confirmed that there was nothing he couldn't tackle. He learned that God would always be there for him. Yet equally important, he learned not to be afraid of problems but rather see them as opportunities to succeed. "I have learned that I'm just here to enjoy the ride. Life will take you where it will take you. When people present me with problems I always think of the opposite and look around the corner to see what's there. Life is a series of opportunities, but opportunities are also challenges, so if you haven't encountered challenges, then you will not have the chance to prevail. You have to seek out these problems, not seek a resistance-free life. Challenges are the best thing in life. I'll always keep looking for challenges." And when you are not afraid of a challenge, you are not afraid of life.

Tim Mitrovich
Government Servant

As we watch a mayor or senator or the president speak, we are seeing the face of our government. They provide facts or opinions or inspiration related to a broad array of issues. Their words and decisions often shape the course of our country and our lives. But they are only the face of our government. Behind them stands the body of government that support them and the institutions and the systems they create. It is the unidentifiable body of men and women who work in the government that make up the lifeblood of government's existence. It is their efforts that breathe life into our government and make it go forward. One such person who loves the world of politics and his country yet stands in the shadows of elected officials is Tim Mitrovich, senior IT specialist in the Office of the Sergeant at Arms, United States Senate. His road to Washington is not much different from that of many others whose only desire is to serve and bring life to their country.

Tim grew up in the world of politics. His father, George Mitrovich, had worked in the presidential campaign of Bobby Kennedy that was cut tragically short by Kennedy's assassination. For five years, the senior Mitrovich worked in the United States Senate as an aide to senators Charles Goodell (R-NY) and Harold Hughes (D-IA). Tim was only eight when the family left Washington for hometown San Diego, but he remembers the impact of having lived in the city of power. He remembers going to work with his father on Capitol Hill and his second-grade class touring the White House of Richard Nixon. The government and politics was all around him. Senators and government leaders coming to dinner was a common occurrence in Washington and San Diego. The conversations around him about world affairs and domestic issues would start to include him as he got older. He came to realize that these giants of government were real people just like him, yet there was something also special about them, which he would later identify as their drive to succeed. Tim talks with excitement about when he was fifteen years old, his father was a delegate for Edward Kennedy's failed attempt for the Democratic nomination. Despite the defeat of his candidate, he remembers walking precincts with his father on behalf of Jimmy Carter and other candidates. With the world of politics and government service all around him, it's no wonder that Tim would start to have thoughts of going into the family business of politics.

Tim's life growing up wasn't all politics. He loved playing high school football and track and feeling like part of a team. He enjoyed great times with his older brother and sister in a family that always seemed to be on the go. By the time he was graduating from high school, like many seniors, he didn't know what he wanted to do as a career. He went to college, changing schools a couple of times and eventually majored in public relations. After graduating, he moved to Boston in search of excitement, but the reality of the difficulty of finding a job and missing his family and girlfriend brought him back to San Diego. He got married and settled into a position in public relations with the San Diego Symphony.

Despite his stated career direction, he still found himself drawn to politics. The drive to return to Washington and to pursue a career in government was strong. Fortunately, his wife was able to get a transfer to a position in Washington, so the newly married couple packed up and moved to the nation's capital in pursuit of Tim's passion. Despite all of the contacts generated by his father, Tim spent over three months seeking a job with an elected official. He finally volunteered in Senator Tom Daschle's office just to get his foot in the door somewhere. In a few weeks, he had proven his value to the office and was given a job in the mail room, managing mail flow. Not exactly what he had in mind, but it was a start.

When Senator Tom Daschle was named to the position as minority leader in the Senate, there was an increase and shift in personnel in the office. As people moved to other positions within the office, opportunities for Tim opened up. He made a point of always letting his bosses know that he wanted to do more. He learned all he could in each job he took on while maintaining good relationships with those around him. As a result of his efforts, he found himself taking on a wide range of assignments, from managing activities in the office to traveling the campaign trail in Senator Daschle's reelection campaign. He was now part of government and politics in all its forms and loving it. One unexpected form came in the form of white power in an envelope. After the attack of 9/11, concerns over terrorism ran high. Fear grew when it was revealed that the deadly chemical anthrax could be condensed into powder form and delivered in mail. One such envelope containing anthrax was delivered to Senator Daschle's office, and Tim was exposed. After weeks of treatment, he was deemed safe, but the reality of the threat of terrorism had its impact on him. Tim started to devise along with others security systems to back up information and to keep governmental employees safe. His job was no longer just about politics and managing data, it became, like all other governmental jobs, about keeping America safe.

Government is about helping people, and while politics is the means of helping people, politics is also about winning and losing. When Tom Daschle lost his reelection bid in 2004, Tim found himself once again looking for a job in Washington. Fortunately, he didn't have to look far or long before an opportunity came to him. The Sergeant of Arms for the United States Senate recognized the skills and experience Tim had in a senator's office and offered him a job handling the technology and information flow within the senate. In reflecting on this move, Tim confesses, "Politics drew me to Washington, but technology keeps me in it."

There are many ways to pursue one's passion while serving your country. Tim will admit that he loves being part of a team and of being "in the game and seeing the fruits of your labor paying off, be it an election, legislation, or whatever." Today, while his job is more "apolitical" in nature, he still feels part of a team, the United States Senate. The lesson of Tim's journey lies in his ability to pursue a passion born in childhood not because of the advantages his father provided him but rather due to his own diligence and willingness to adjust to the opportunities before him in the pursuit of serving his country.

> *Ask not what your country can do for you,*
> *Ask what you can do for your country.*
> *—President John F. Kennedy*

Jeffery Wood
Blind Fury

Across America, young boys and girls are playing baseball with the neighborhood kids. Jeff started playing when he was four years old. He and the kids of the neighborhood played constantly. His father even built a backstop to keep the Whiffle balls from going into the neighbor's yard. As Jeff got older, he played Little League with his father being the coach and his mother being active in the league. Jeff would be on the field from morning to night. When the baseball season was over, he would go play soccer. Being athletic and busy was just the way it was with Jeff. If it wasn't athletics, it was studying for school. He was always on the go, and his friendly manner made him a favorite with peers and adults alike. Everyone liked Jeff Wood.

It was his junior year in high school and the tryouts for the Steele Canyon Varsity baseball team. Jeff had excelled at every level he had played, and now he was preparing to do the same when he noticed that he was having trouble seeing the ball in the air. He quickly called his mother to bring up another pair of contact lenses, but the result was the same. His optometrist reported that he could only correct Jeff's vision to 20/40, and he was referred to what would become a series of doctors and tests. Jeff spent all of spring break in the hospital being tested; all this time, his vision got worse. First his left eye and then his right eye became ever increasingly blurred. He remembers being confused and thinking, *Will my vision ever improve?* He could hear the emotional strain in voices of his mother, father, and younger sister even though they continued to try to appear positive. By May, it was determined that he had Leber's disease, a rare mitochondria disease that affects one in three thousand. Due to a dying off cells in the optic nerve, centralized vision is lost, leaving only the peripheral vision intact. Jeff had gone from having perfect 20/20 vision in March to 20/200 in June and being legally blind. He still can relive the shock he felt when his doctor told him that there was no cure and it might get worse.

The shock of coming to grips with going blind as a sixteen-year-old was hard not only on Jeff, but also on family and friends. His parents, who are teachers, would try to remain strong and positive for him. His mother remembers going to work on automatic pilot, dreading the return home each day out of a fear that Jeff's eyesight had deteriorated even more. Her coworkers felt her pain and organized to raise money for the family so they could go on a trip before Jeff was totally blind. Word of Jeff's plight filtered down to the elementary school where he had attended and his mother was so active. The staff of that school, using a fundraising program that had been started years before by his mother, started to raise money on Jeff's behalf. An FBI agent in the area heard of Jeff and donated his time-share in Hawaii for a trip as well as arranged for a tour of the White House. So with the start of summer Jeff and his family went to Hawaii and swam with the turtles. When they returned, the family accompanied his father to New York were he was to attend a conference. They went on to Washington and then Boston, where Jeff got his wish to sit on the Green Monster in Fenway Park and watch a Yankee-Red Sox game. Even though his vision continued to deteriorate, Jeff admits that he was being kept too busy to think about what was happening or the eventual consequences.

While family and friends rallied around Jeff, there was something else that contributed to pulling him through this rough time: running track. With baseball being no longer an option, Jeff looked down on the track below the baseball field and wondered. He had always been one of the fastest kids he played with, could he run track? He approached Charles Tyler, the track coach and friend of Jeff's father about running for Steele Canyon. Coach Tyler's response was "I hope you are faster than your father." So started a relationship with the coaches and track that would give new meaning to Jeff's life. Coach Tyler was supportive, but he expected from Jeff the same as he did everyone else, especially as Jeff became one of the leading sprinters on the team. Jeff would later say, "I fell in love with track and the dedication that is required to the sport. Your mind has to be focused for every part of the race, every part of practice. You can't half ass anything." Besides the love of running, deep friendships emerged such as Tony Smith, with whom Jeff would work hours to perfect the baton handoff in the relays. It was Tony who nicknamed Jeff "Blind Fury," a name that Jeff now has tattooed on his left arm. Jeff was determined to get faster and to continue track in college.

Jeff was not only a gifted athlete; he was also a gifted student, graduating from Steele Canyon with a 4.42 grade point average. He had always been focused on going to college, and even with the loss of his sight, his goal had not changed. He had to learn how to use new devises that would help him to see the printed word. He remembers during his junior year, as his eyesight decreased daily, not trusting the assistive devises, relying instead on a magnifying glass to read and study for his finals in AP calculus, AP English, and AP history. During breaks in his school schedule, he would attend classes for the blind to learn more about how to use the reading devises. It was after grudgingly giving up his spring break in his senior year to attend such a class that he received word that he had been accepted to the University of Southern California. His state rehabilitation worker counseled him to take it slowly and to start at a junior college, but taking it slowly is not Jeff's approach to things, so he left San Diego for USC, over 150 miles away from home . . . alone.

Jeff admits that he doesn't like being in large crowds, and USC is a big school. He struggled at first with adapting to the demands, but so did the school struggle to adapt to him. The disabilities department at USC was not familiar with how to meet Jeff's needs at first, but with the persistent advocacy of his mother, Jeff eventually received the latest in assistive technology designed to enlarge the font of textbooks and the font on his computer. Jeff has had to deal with the devices breaking down at times, from which he has learned the importance of being his own advocate. Yet the classroom was not the only area Jeff learned to assert himself; he also went out for and made the USC track team. His dedication to his education and to track became evident to everyone who met him. As a result of being the person and athlete that he is, Jeff became a Swim with Mike scholarship winner, which will pay for his entire schooling at USC.

Today, Jeff's eyesight has stabilized to 20/800, and he will tell you that losing his sight was "one of the best things that happened to me, it gave me a lot of structure to my life. I don't think I would be at USC if it hadn't happened." While giving credit to his family and friends for their constant support, this kinesiology major admits that the hardest part of being visually impaired "is having to ask for help for so many things." His mother admits that the hardest part for her has been not to rescue him from the challenges at USC but rather let him find his own way to cope. Jeff also identifies his emerging faith in God and his love of track as a source of his strength. "Track has kept me focused 100 percent because I know I am competing with a visioned world so I have to be climbing the stairs a little faster than everyone else." He recognizes that he has lost such things as being able to drive and playing baseball, but before heading to the beach to try surfing for the first time, he said, "You just have to add things to your life to balance it out." He will admit to getting discouraged at times, but never did he think he would not succeed. "I never felt I would get so worn out, tired, or fatigued that I would give up. I just feel like I'm in a race that will never end, so I might as well keep on running ahead, trying to win." In a television interview conducted while Jeff was still at Steele Canyon, his track coach Charles Tyler may have given the best description of Jeff:

> He sees the bigger picture better than a lot of kids and I think he will make the most of his opportunities from now on instead of a lot of other kids, they don't have that sight.

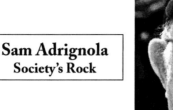

Sam Adrignola
Society's Rock

All around the world, you will find families coming together to eat and share in the common bond of family. At the head of many of these dinners sits the patriarch of the family proudly watching the evolution of life playing out before him. Such a family can be found most weekend nights in a small neighborhood of San Diego called Kensington. At the head of the table sits the patriarch listening to four generations sharing, debating, and supporting one another. He says very little, yet hears and understands everything. He is the father, the father-in-law, the papa to those at the table. There are those seated who see him for what he is and may know little of his journey through life. They know him only as the incredibly wise, eternally positive, and unconditionally accepting constant in the evolution of the family. Yet this is only part of this man. There is more to his life experiences that needs to be known to truly understand and appreciate the depth of the man.

Sam Adrignola is eldest son of Italian immigrants raised along with his two younger brothers and one sister in Rockford, Illinois. It was the time of the Great Depression, and Italians at the time were seen as an inferior minority characterized by a strong back and low intelligence. Work was hard to find for his father, which meant that the family was on welfare and often went without the basic necessities. Sam would go to school barefoot most of the time and, in the winter, would get boots from welfare. Sam relates that he didn't know he was poor because everyone else was poor. He remembers one Christmas seated around the table with his brothers and sister, watching their father trying to carve the only food they had, a head of cabbage. He will never forget the silent pain in his father's face as he tried to slice the cabbage into equal parts. Sam's father was a proud man who wanted to provide more for his family yet only felt more humiliated with each slice. In a sudden rage, he picked up the cabbage and threw half of it out the window. Sam remembers the silence, no one daring to speak. The silence was suddenly broken by a knock at the door. It was people from the welfare department bringing a Christmas basket of food and toys. Sam watched as his parents graciously accepted the charity, all the time knowing that his father was dying inside.

In school, Sam was a good student, but he knew that he never could afford going to college, so he enrolled in vocational classes. He was especially good at drafting, and upon graduating, he searched for a job in drafting. With the help of his vocational teacher, he got a job working in a shop for 35¢ an hour. While this was better than the 35¢-50¢ a day he had earned since he was twelve years old working as a caddy, after three months, he demanded a raise. His boss wouldn't meet his demand, but he did refer him to a tool-and-die shop, and there he was hired for 91¢ an hour. Being an apprentice was quite an honor since he was the first Italian American in town allowed to work in the tool-and-die industry. There he would work for three years until World War II broke out. Soon after the start of the war, Sam wanted to volunteer in the army air corps. He was accepted, but could not enlist without the permission of his boss due to the critical nature of his job. His boss refused to release him, so Sam refused to work. After four hours of Sam sitting and doing nothing, his boss relented, and Sam started his journey in the United States Army Air Corps.

His experience in the military started with aptitude tests and prolonged months of training. Sam scored at the top of all of the tests, which only fueled his dreams of being a pilot. Sam remembers in great detail being called into the commanding officer's office and the complete conversation:

> Officer: Mr. Adrignola, we think you would make a good navigator.
>
> Sam: I want to be a pilot, sir.
>
> Officer: We think with your scores, you would be a very good navigator.
>
> Sam: With all due respect, sir, I would like to be a pilot.
>
> Officer: Let me put it to you this way. You can go to navigator school or you can wash out.
>
> Sam: Sir, I think I would be a good navigator.

So with this settled, Sam started months of one school after another. He finally got his wings on July 7, 1945, and was stationed at the army air base in San

Marcos, Texas, as a navigation instructor. Now that he had a secure station, he and his childhood sweetheart, Anna Tangora decided to get married. He had first spotted Anna at a basketball game. She was rooting for the team he was playing, and throughout the game, he showed off, trying to get her to notice him. That night, he did meet her and now, years later, she was preparing to board a train to Texas to marry Sam. A week before she was to arrive, the squadron orderly came to the flight line and told him to report to the commander's office immediately. He was told that he was placed on special orders. He was to pack and be ready to move out at a moment's notice. The orders had come directly from Washington and were top secret. He was to tell no one, not even his future bride. He made up a story to Anna about flying out for a few days, and so he wouldn't be able to call her. He then sat and waited to be shipped out to an unknown assignment or to meet his fiancé's train. A few days before Anna was to arrive, and a day after the first atomic bomb landed on Hiroshima, Sam was released from his orders. It turned out that General Jimmy Doolittle wanted a crew available to drop the first atomic bomb on Tokyo, and Sam was to be the navigator. As it turned out, instead of dropping the bomb to end a war, he met a train to start the greatest achievement of his life.

World War II ended soon after the atomic bomb was dropped, and Sam returned to Rockford with Anna and resumed his career as a tool and die maker. Yet civilian life didn't last long with the breakout of the Korean War. Sam was quickly retrained and assigned to the 343rd Bomb Squadron, 98th Bomb Group stationed at Yakota AFB, Japan flying in a B-29 named Miss Minooki. He would fly in fifty-four combat missions in the ship whose nose was adorned with an artful rendering of the scantly clad Miss Minooki. Of all of the missions, the one on April 14, 1951, is forever etched on Sam's memory. It was on this day during a normal bombing run that the crew of Miss Minooki met with unusually strong antiaircraft fire. Shells were bursting all around them, but it was not the shells outside they had to worry about; it was the one inside. One of the bombs in the forward bay had failed to release and now dangled by one shackle. Fortunately, it was the same shackle that would arm the bomb, so there was no explosion yet. For the next two hours on their flight back to base over open waters, the crew tried to release the bomb, but with no success. As Miss Minooki made her descent, the crew said their final prayers, not knowing if with the change in altitude would make the bomb ignite. They made their final turn to land when suddenly, the bomb broke loose from the shackle and harmlessly fell in a rice paddy below, three miles from the end of the runway. Miss Minooki and her crew, who had melded into one, had survived to fly and fight again.

Not only had the crew melded with Miss Minooki, so had the wives of the crew. The wives didn't have regular communication with their husbands, and to help with the days of worry, they had come to know one another well. One night, Anna had a dream that Miss Minooki had crashed and all were gone. She awoke in a sweat from her nightmare and, in the morning, called Ellie, wife of the pilot, for comfort. Instead of comfort, Anna learned that Ellie too had the same dream. That day, it was reported that a B-29 had crashed in the Sea of Japan with no survivors. Ellie eventually got a call from her husband explaining that it was Miss Minooki who crashed, but that he, Sam, and the rest of the crew were not on board at the time. It turned out that another crew took the great lady up for an additional bombing run at night and had run out of fuel and crashed. Shortly afterward, the Korean War ended, and once again, Sam returned to civilian life and his family.

Sam once again returned to his job as a tool and die maker in Rockford, but it wasn't long before he concluded that he was getting nowhere in his career and was open to a change. Anna's parents and family had moved to San Diego, and she missed them deeply. So Sam and Anna sold their house and, with their two kids, went west to unite the family. Filled with confidence, Sam hit the streets to find a job. The first day he searched, he was hired as a tool and die maker in the experimental department at Ryan Aeronautical where he would work for the next thirty-five years. Sam always wanted a challenge, and to learn more, so he went to San Diego State and studied engineering as he moved up the ranks at Ryan. It wasn't easy working all day and studying all night, but it was what it took. His family grew right along with his career. He and Anna had five children and later adopted a sixth. To Sam, his family always came first. The family was very tightly knit with traditions and love, yet everyone had their own life going in different directions. One morning, Sam's children were to wake up to find that their father had been up all night watching the coverage of the Lunar Landing Module setting down on the surface of the moon. When asked why he was so interested, his only response was, "I helped build it." Sam was a director of a design team when Ryan was contracted to design the antenna for the lunar landing module. The specifications were vague, and the techniques needed to create the antenna proved to not yet have been invented. The problem was that the antenna had to not only be able to transmit and receive radio communication, it also had to be durable and lightweight. The solution Sam felt was to combine magnesium with one percent of zirconium. The problem was that brazing them together required very exact temperatures, which had never been done before. NASA scientists, engineers across the country, and even the president of Ryan said it couldn't be done, yet the old tool and die maker and his design team felt it could be done. Now his family would learn what he had been doing at work, and a nation would once again reap the benefits.

When Sam retired from Ryan, his family, for Christmas, bought him remote control model plane kits so he would have a hobby. While gracious in receiving the gift, he returned them the next day. His hobby in retirement has been to find ways to improve as many lives as possible. He got active in the Italian American service club, UNICO, and helped raise thousands of dollars for charities and scholarships. Every Saturday morning, he meets with a group of men from a variety of careers and political persuasions to share, laugh, and discuss the issues of the day. The Kensington coffee group has become legendary and is frequently visited by local politicians and even national figures such as George Dukakis, all seeking honest talk. While the group has been known to get loud, resulting in having been kicked out of two coffeehouses when there is a hot political disagreement, "Sam the Saint," as one article described him will bring understanding and acceptance through his calm and thoughtful words.

Sam's life has spanned and touched the most significant events of his generation. He lived through the Great Depression, fought in two wars, and helped put man on the moon; yet these are not of which he is proudest. He will tell you if asked that his greatest success in life is "my marriage and raising my kids." He will tell you that he has had self-doubt and has made mistakes. Yet he believes through prayer, persistence, and honesty with yourself that you will find the solution. To his family, he is Papa, the head of the family who gives unconditional love and support. To our society, Sam and the fathers and mothers like him serve as the rock of the family that does what must be done to keep the family rolling on.

To those who have met him, he is like the heat lamp that brightens your world and warms your being. And to all of mankind, he is the symbol of what is the best that is in all of us, the best we can strive to be.

How to Develop the Qualities and Talents of Successful People

*The will to win is not as important as the
will to prepare to win.*

—Unknown

Success is not an inherited trait; it is a learned behavior. A baby does not instinctually know how to walk or talk; they are taught how to do so through observation and copying others. A baseball player may have inherited a strong muscular body, but he has to learn how to control his swing to hit the curve ball. A person could have experienced repeated failures, but having learned from each failure eventually changes how they do something and become a success. Success is not limited to those who are blessed with it; it is limited to those who will work to obtain it. Everyone wants to be successful. I'm sure you have heard people give great descriptions of what they want to achieve, but years later, they are still talking about it or about what might have been. They can recite in great depth all the obstacles or bad luck that kept them from achieving their desired goal. Some will say that they really didn't want to do that after all and it's no big deal. Whatever the explanation, the truth is that they wanted it, but didn't do it. Successful people are doers. They act upon their dreams and goals and not just talk about them. They are not afraid of taking the risk to fail, but rather, are more afraid of not trying to succeed. Successful people take action to pursue and put in motion their goals and dreams. Taking action is the key to developing the qualities and talents of successful people.

This may sound strange, but before jumping further into the "how to" of becoming successful, take time to assess if you really want to be successful.

There are advantages to setting goals, of having dreams and never pursuing them. Remember what I said previously:

- We choose what we do
- Everything we do makes sense at the time we do it
- We do it because the advantages outweigh the disadvantages.

Stop and think for a while. What are the advantages of not succeeding? What are the advantages of not losing weight, of not passing a class, of not asking that girl you're attracted to on a date? Your first reaction may be to say that there are no reasons. That is what a patient of mine said who sought therapy with the intent of losing weight. She was sure there were no reasons why she would want to be so overweight. After forty-five minutes, we had a list of over twenty reasons why someone would want to be overweight. We came up with such things as (1) being overweight you could eat anything and it wouldn't show, (2) she didn't have to worry about men picking up on her thus tempting her to cheat on her husband, (3) she didn't have to live up to the expectation of the slender successful businesswomen in their fitted suits, (4) and she was so overweight that it would be unhealthy for her to have a child, which she really didn't want to have. After making the list, I told her to go home and think about if she really wanted to lose weight and tell me the next week. When she returned the following week, she was dressed better than I had ever seen her, and her makeup was perfect. When she sat down, I asked her what she had decided. She responded with, "I've decided to not lose weight." Therapy was over. She had decided that she liked being who and what she was and didn't need to beat herself up any longer trying to lose weight. Many people lose weight to feel better about themselves when actually, you need to feel better about yourself to lose weight. My patient was now more ready to lose weight than ever before, but the advantages to not lose weight outweighed the advantages to go on a diet and change her lifestyle.

With each goal comes unique reasons why not to pursue success, but also can be found are some basic universal reasons to avoid success. The first most mentioned is the fear that you might fail. No one likes failing, but failing may be necessary to point you in the direction of success. It can be as important to know what doesn't work as it is to know what does work. Yet it is not the potential embarrassment of failing that deters people as much as it is the fear of the responsibility that comes with succeeding. As stated in the Spiderman movies, "With great powers come great responsibilities." Once you have succeeded, you are expected to do so again. People look to you to maintain the level you have achieved and to serve as inspiration to them. Yet being successful is not just about the responsibility one has toward others, but also to themselves. When you strive to succeed, you are taking responsibility for yourself. You are not deferring to or blaming others for the outcome. You are saying, "I will do this and I'm willing to accept whatever are the consequences, good and bad, of my actions." This does not mean you are fearless, but rather, you are motivated to move forward despite your fears. Such courage to succeed is necessary before the steps to succeed can be taken.

In this section of the book, you will be presented with ideas and some concrete ways you can train yourself to be successful. While you will be shown what is involved and how to do it, it will be up to you to do it. Before you can become successful, you have to first, want to succeed, and then take action to succeed.

> *All dreams can come true, if we have the*
> *courage to pursue them.*
> *—Walt Disney*

How to Find the Commitment of Successful People

*When you discover your mission, you will
feel its demand. It will fill you with enthusiasm
and a burning desire to get to work on it.*
—*W. Clement Stone*

The key to finding what you are committed to lies in identifying what you are passionate about. It is easy to commit our time, our energy, our life to that which we are passionate about and brings meaning and definition to our lives. We all are faced with the universal question of "Why am I here on earth?" The very asking of this question spawns other questions like "Am I getting everything I should out of my life?" "What is important in life?" and "Am I happy?" The road to finding one's passion is paved with many questions. For some in life, they seem to fall into what is their passion. For them, there is very little doubt that they are doing what brings them joy. They are the fortunate ones because for the majority of people, they must seek out their passion through observation, experience, and self-reflection.

Talk shows and motivational speakers challenge and often chastise us to seek our true passion. To leave the job we hate for the riches and glory of pursuing our dreams. Leave behind the shackles of the daily grind for the fresh air of freedom and self-actualization. That may be a romantic and positive message to sell, but not everyone sees themselves in a position to buy it. You may want to buy the pursuit of your passion, but your needs dictate a different course. Abraham Maslow wrote about man having a hierarchy of needs that he characterized in the form of a pyramid. At the bottom of the pyramid are the physiological needs, followed by the safety and security needs, the love and belonging needs, and the esteem needs near the top. He referred to these as deficit needs, which we are motivated to obtain. At the tip of the pyramid is what he called self-actualization, which is a state where you are becoming the most complete and fullest you can be. To achieve this state, you must have satisfied the needs below. When you are struggling to get your physiological needs and safety and security needs met, it is hard to focus on issues of self-esteem and the pursuit of your passion. Survival takes precedence over finding meaning. So it becomes clearer why seeking one's passion is more likely found in cultures where the basic needs are more readily met.

Having acknowledged there are legitimate reasons that might hinder seeking one's passion, there are also many excuses posed as reasons to not change one's direction in life. The excuses include the following:

- *Overwhelmed with obligations.* For the single mother of five children who lives from paycheck to paycheck, this may be a legitimate reason to not pursue your passion. Yet one's pursuit of their passion need not be expensive or time consuming. It may actually serve as a balance in a day and a life that seems to be too much to bear. Taking small islands of time to pursue one's love for woodworking, writing, or studying may not only renew you and get you closer to your ultimate goal, but will also make you no longer feel trapped. Remember, J. K. Rowling was a single mother of two on welfare when she conceived of and wrote the first of the Harry Potter books.

- *Trapped.* You are only trapped if you choose to see yourself as trapped. While you may feel a prisoner of your situation, your mind is always free. The thinking of and pursuing of your passion in even a limited way will break you free.

- *No energy after meeting obligations.* While this is a legitimate factor, the involvement in your passion, even on a limited basis, may give you energy.

- *Focus on pleasing others rather than what is best for themselves.* While placing others needs above your own is noble and may actually be your passion, it also serves as a means to avoid taking responsibility for your own life. Focusing only on others means you never have to state what you want, right or wrong. Such people often feel it is safer to say and do nothing rather than be criticized.

- *Fear.* Fear of the unknown, fear of failure, and fear of taking a risk have kept many a person on the sideline of life just watching the game and not participating in it. It's not that they don't want to be in the game, but when fear creeps in, so do scenarios of failure. The obstacles become bigger and "what if" consumes their mind. "What if I can't learn it?" "What if those involved don't like me?" "What if I fail?"

- *Self-doubt.* Self-doubt is related to fear and focuses on your personal inadequacies. You start to question your own skills and potential, which leads to your imagining and believing that you are a failure, so why try.

- *Paralysis.* Paralysis occurs when you become confused or uncertain, thus preventing yourself from making a change. You can't do the wrong thing if you do nothing . . . or can you! Passion is the stimulant to jolt you out of your paralysis, but you have to let go to let it happen.

- *Numbness.* When the daily routine, demands, and stresses of life become a blur, numbing can take place. You don't feel pleasure or pain, just an emotional disconnectedness and apathy toward life. It can become so numbing that you are not even aware that you are unhappy and missing out on the thrill of passion.
- *Limited scope.* Labels such as male or female, Afro-American, Hispanic or Caucasian, and young or old help to identify us but don't say who we are as a person. If these are accepted as the boundaries of our potentials, then we limit ourselves to a stereotyped existence.
- *Procrastination.* It is not that the procrastinator doesn't want to pursue their passion, it's that they set up criteria that keeps them from pursuing it. Things such as "I will quit my job when I have enough money" or "I will take dancing lessons when I have enough time." Do you ever have enough money or time? They set up A dependent on B statements. I will do A if B occurs, but since B won't occur, I'll never do A.
- *Caution.* Being controlled and calculating is not a bad thing, until it interferes with taking the risk necessary to ignite passion. An element of passion is the excitement of risk and eliminating the chance of failure may also suppress the success of releasing your passion.
- *Mind over heart.* Logic and analysis are crucial to success. While they serve as the engine of the car, passion is the gas that makes the car go.
- *Afraid to dream.* We all want our dreams to come true, but the fear of being disappointed often keeps us from dreaming.

These excuses are the thicket we must push through if we are to find and pursue our passion. Yet before one embarks on their coveted prize, it helps to know what is the prize. What is it that you are passionate enough about to overcome the obstacles to maintain the status quo? What will motivate you enough to take the risk to fulfill your potential?

Finding Your Passion

I frequently hear "I don't know what I'm passionate about" or "If I only knew what was my passion I would pursue it." Not knowing is a frequent reason for not doing, but it doesn't have to be. Some people travel the world in their search to find the answers to such important questions. In reality, you don't have to even leave your seat to find your passion. You just have to be observant and willing to under go some self-assessment. This is because while what you are passionate about may lie outside you, the identification of that passion lies within you. Imbedded in your behavior, feelings, and beliefs is your passion waiting to be discovered. You just have to ask the right questions to reveal it.

An initial question you can ask yourself is "What is valuable to me?" What may have first come to your mind were probably people, objects, or experiences in your world. Your children, money, your team winning the Super Bowl—these are what we hold dear and strive to have in our lives. These are the things that we value and gain some identity from, but they are not who we are and what motivates us. That comes from the values inside us that influence all of our decisions. Values are the standards of desirability by which we choose between alternative behaviors. Every decision has some direct purpose and value, which is at the root of that decision. Values provide the standards by which attitudes are formed about the world around us. Values are formed through our relationships growing up and our experiences throughout life. Values are at the core of who we are and why we do what we do. When we become so certain, so emotionally in tune with one value or group of values that we are moved to take action, we have reached the level of commitment to that value. Values can be motivating factors in determining goals and provide personal definition for successful achievement and serve as a reference point for self-worth. By being able to identify and understand your values, you will receive a valuable clue into what are the components that makes up your passion.

For those who are not sure what they value, what motivates them, and what they are passionate about, I suggest you take the time to ask yourself some questions. I have listed below possible questions that, when answered, may reveal to you the direction you seek. The list is long and may seem repetitive, but I have found that essentially the same question worded in a slightly different manner may stimulate a different response. Some of the questions may stimulate immediate responses, while others may need more time and reflection to answer. Many of the questions are based upon what you or others have observed about your behavior. Others elicit what you think or believe, which again may be construed from your actions as well as your thoughts. You may also notice that behind your answers lies a glimpse into your basic underlying values. I suggest that you write down your answers or free associations to the questions. You may want to add to or change your responses after having time to reflect. You may find that the question motivates you to investigate something further. Just be open to letting the questions lead you where they will.

Ask yourself the following:

What makes me happy?
What gets me excited?
What seems to energize me?
What was I passionate about as a child?
What was I good at as a child?

What are my talents?

What skills can I perform?

What parts of the jobs I've held do I enjoy?

What do I like doing?

What do I never tire doing?

What can't I get enough of?

What is my vision of a perfect vocational day?

What am I willing to sacrifice and take risks for?

What do I feel I just have to do?

What do I identify with?

How do I want to be viewed?

Am I doing what I feel?

Am I in an environment where I can flourish?

What do I dream of?

Who do I admire?

Who do I know that's doing something I'd like to do? (Describe yourself doing it.)

Who would I like to be?

What is my purpose in life?

What would I do if I knew I could not fail?

What do I love about myself?

What would I do if money was not a concern in my life?

What do I fantasize about doing while driving my car or taking a shower?

How could I make the world a better place for myself and others?

When I was young, what did I know I would do when I grow up?

What would I regret not having done if my life was ending?

After answering a number of these questions, you may still be unclear as to the direction you should take. You may find that you are attracted to more than one passion in your life. It is common to have multiple passions; you just have to learn how to prioritize and balance them. You may have a passion for sailing, but you have to balance it with your passion to provide for your family. All of nature is about balance. Stress is the lack of balance. Pursuing your passion does not mean divorcing yourself from the demands of your daily life. Opening yourself up to pursuing in at least a portion of your life that which you are passionate about may be the nourishment you need to get through your day. It is like paying creditors. If you are always paying everyone else and never give some money to yourself, you will never feel like you are getting ahead and may get discouraged and worn out. Striking the proper balance allows you to have more energy to better meet the challenges of your day. In addition, finding the proper balance in your life will allow you the freedom to pursue your passion.

Maybe you have identified a few things you could get passionate about, but you just don't know which one to pursue. In this case, you can do a couple of things. First, look at what you have identified as your possible passions and see what are the common elements between them. You may like working with the elderly, coaching little league, and being active in fighting global warming. Let's say while you try to balance these pursuits, you really have time to focus on only one. In deciding which one to pursue, it might be helpful to recognize that they all have some common elements. They all involve being social and making a difference in other people's lives. This may constitute that the passion and the location to express the passion may not be as important. Where it is expressed may be the result of availability and opportunity. As long as you are making a difference, you are happy. Another way to narrow down your list of which passion you should pursue is to take each of them out for a test drive. Get involved in what you identified and see if you like it. Examine what is involved. Do you get energized by doing it, do you like identifying with it? One car may drive well, but you like the color of the next one better, and you feel good when driving it, so you buy the second car. As you learn more, you narrow down your choices. Why should we not be as analytical and discriminating when choosing the course of our lives as we are choosing our car?

If after all of this analysis you still find yourself unable to define your passion, stop, relax, and let your unconscious speak to you. Because you are focusing on the issue of finding your passion, your unconscious is working on and possibly even solving the problem for you. The unfortunate thing is that we often are not sensitive to listening to what it is saying to us through our dreams and what we discard as random thoughts and feelings. Thomas Edison, the famous inventor, was noted for dozing off when working on a design or problem. He would awaken from his short catnaps with the solution to his dilemma. When relaxed and the mind was clear, the unconscious was able to provide him the answers he was seeking. The unconscious is the source of all problem solving and healing. Learning to relax and listen to your intuition may actually turn on the streetlamps on your road to success.

Meaning, Values, Passion, and Commitment

I've been talking a lot about the importance of finding your passion, but to really answer the big question "What is my purpose in life?" you have to understand the relationship between meaning, values, passion, and commitment. Meaning in life has been sought throughout the ages. Crusades have been launched in quest of it, and poets have written riddles to try to explain it. To answer the question "Who am I?" one must answer, "In relation to what?" We do not live in a vacuum, but rather, in a world in which we gain definition from our values being exposed and shaped by the physical, social, and psychological world around us. In the end, it is not a place or a thing, but rather, a state of being. The integration of value, belief, need, desire, and hope into one very personal realization that this is who I am and what I'm all about. While it is about the individual, it takes form not inside the person, but rather, in the "investment made in someone or some thing beyond yourself," as Victor Frankl would say. Meaning is about submerging who you are into a world that gives you a stage upon which to display your being and give it validation. Passion is the drive stemming from your values, that gives you the courage to risk being part of the dance between meaning and who you are. Passion leads or drives us to that place of meaning and purpose in life. Commitment is the discipline required to take the journey. When the beacon of meaning and the electricity of passion are strong, it makes commitment easier, but not effortless.

Ideally you find yourself passionate about something that brings meaning and purpose into your life, and you are committed to pursuing it. Using the car analogy again, values account for the type of car; meaning is the engine; passion, the spark plug; and commitment, the fuel that propels the car. Note that while value and meaning give the car definition, and passion starts the engine, it is commitment that keeps the car running. It takes effort to experience meaning and to express a passion. Knowing what floats your boat is not enough to get it away from the dock. It takes action. It takes action in the form of a commitment to reaching the goal and to producing meaning. You have to be committed to take the steps necessary to live your life as you want it to be. Often you hear that if you just visualize what you desire that it will come to you. While seeing clearly what you seek is important, it is not enough to just wish for it. You have to work to get it. You have to be willing to take the risks and to welcome change. You have to do what successful people do to be successful. You have to develop and learn to play your cards as do the successful people.

Strategies to Find the Winning Commitment

- *What Do I Value in Life (exercise 1).* Underlying and deeply woven into what we are passionate about, find meaning in, and commit to are what we value the most. Going against what we value takes the enjoyment and purpose out of what we are doing while shaping our commitments around what we value supplies a continuing confirmation of our identity. In the appendix, you will find exercise 1, What I Value in Life, which consists of twenty-one different values, along with their definition, which you are to rate as to their level of importance for you. You are then to identify which you would rate as your five most highly held values and which would be your five lowest-held values.

- *Value Comparison Inventory (exercise 2)*. This exercise, which involves comparing the relative relationship between values. Utilizing the value definitions found in exercise 1, you are to rank five different values against one another until all of the combinations of values have been ranked. You are then to total the score received for each value to determine the relative strength of each value for you.

- *Finding Your Definition of Success (exercise 3)*. In this exercise, you are to identify the instances when you felt successful at various times in your life and then analyze those success experiences for the qualities which made you feel successful. Being able to identify the qualities that make up the success experience will allow you to guide your life into activities where you will receive similar benefits.

- *Creating Your Mission Statement (exercise 4)*. Corporations, organizations, or any program or project, before starting to do what is to be done, writes a mission statement. This is a clear and concise statement as to what is the purpose and intent of the activities that are about to be pursued. The preamble to the United States Constitution is a mission statement of the purpose and intent of the government. Write your own mission statement for your life. What is your purpose in life and how do you intend to pursue that purpose? Writing such a statement will give you a sense of direction and a point to which to refer to during your life to assess if you are staying on course.

If one advances confidently in the direction of his dreams,
and endeavors to live the life which has imagined,
he will meet with a success unexpected in common hours.
—*Henry David Thoreau*

How to Learn the Attitude of Successful People

The greatest discovery of any generation is that
a human being can alter his life by altering
his attitude.
—*William James*

A positive "can do" spirit may be the attitude of successful people, but the mystery that follows is "Where does it come from and how do you obtain it?" You are not born with an attitude that "failure is not an option." It does not grow on trees. It does not come from a pill you take. Such an attitude is not given to you; you are taught such an attitude. It is taught by your parents when you were young, and if not then, by those with whom you surround yourself when you are older. The development of the drive to succeed is a learned behavior.

Motivation to Succeed

The first teachers of the attitude of success were your parents. Ideally you had parents that were hard-working high achievers who served as role models of the importance of education and succeeding. They encouraged you to be independent and let you set your own goals and make your own mistakes. Sure they communicated to you that they had high goals for you, but they were realistic goals, always taking into account your abilities at the time. They never pushed you too much, but always encouraged you to do your best. They sang your praises and gave help when you needed it. They encouraged you to think for yourself and to dream your own dreams, not do it their way or take on their dreams for you. They taught you the importance of rules, self-discipline, and shared responsibilities. Basically, they provided you a home where you felt loved, secure, valued, and respected. If you come from such a home, you have probably learned and internalized a certain drive to achieve. It has been bred into you to seek more, to achieve more.

For those who were not so lucky as to have the "perfect parents," you may have to understand what is "achievement motivation" before you can develop it in yourself. You have probably heard of those who took great risks on the stock market or in a business and became rich and thought to yourself, *I could never be so successful because I couldn't take such risks.* Sure there is some risk taking necessary in succeeding. "You can't steal second base and keep your foot on first." Yet it is a myth to believe that achievement-oriented people are gamblers or risk takers. In fact, high achievement-oriented people seek out a balanced challenge in which a task is not too easy and not impossible. Let's say you wanted to become a gourmet chef. You find a recipe for pheasant under glass, and you decide to prepare it. The only problem is that you don't know how to boil water, let alone cook a pheasant. This would not be a goal of a truly achievement-oriented person, but rather a delusional optimist. Achievement-oriented people are realistic. They set goals that they can influence with their effort and ability while at the same time is achievable. A truly achievement-oriented person would start with learning how to cook scrambled eggs and work their way up to pheasant. For such people, achieving their aim or task is more important than receiving praise or recognition. Their drive to seek ways of dong things better further promotes the view that such people make things happen and achieve goals.

If achieving is about a drive to succeed, then it is important to understand that drive is the combination of the answer to three basic questions:

1. What do I want or need?
2. What are the odds that I can get it?
3. What's in it for me?

Within us are a number of competing wants and needs. The need to speak up for yourself in a relationship may be competing with the fear of losing the relationship. The desire to excel in school may be competing with a desire to not be noticed or viewed as an egghead. The hope for success is often in conflict with the fear of failure, making the behavior dependent upon whichever becomes dominate. It is the identity and strength of these wants and needs that give purpose to what we seek.

What the odds are that you can achieve your goal are based upon your past experience of succeeding or failing. If you have the skills and have been successful at building garages, you are more likely to believe that you can build a house. The more familiar you are with a task or similar tasks, the more optimistic you will be that you'll succeed again. The expectation that the task can be achieved is a major contributor to the confidence of successful people.

The final factor in drive or motivation is "what's in it for me?" The incentive we feel to pursue a goal depends upon how badly we want a certain payoff at that time. It may be worth putting up with a "sabertooth boss" to get a comfortable salary, but if your health is failing due to the stress, that paycheck may be less attractive. You could say that the greater the rewards, the more appealing it will be to pursue a goal, but what is considered appealing for one person may hold no motivation for another.

By finding the answer to theses three questions when considering a goal, you will be identifying what fuels your motivation to achieve the goal.

All of the above-mentioned factors which contribute to a person's drive to succeed are learned and, therefore, can be trained. It would be nice if everyone could be parented or reparented in a supportive, positive home with high yet realistic expectations and mutual respect. Unfortunately, these are not the cards some people are dealt. But as an adult, you can seek out groups and environments where such interactions between one another do take place. The more you associate with positive people, the more positive you will become. The more you see mutual respect being given, the more you will believe it is possible and that you deserve being treated that way. As you grow to trust that environment more, the more relaxed you will become and the less defensive you will be about taking risks to try something new or challenging. As you feel more supported, the wanting to succeed will be more socially acceptable to you. That old mother's proverb, "you are who you associate with," is true because who you associate with influences what you think, and what you think is who you are.

Being in positive, supportive environments is desirable, yet there are those who would not recognize such a place even if they crashed into it while speeding down the highway of life. Many such people can't see the positive that is around them because they are too focused on the pain within them. These people we call depressed. A depressed person filters everything through a dark window in their mind that distorts and transforms what is seen into the negative. For such people, everything is twisted and interpreted in such terms as "I can't win," "They are out to get me," and "I'm inadequate and a failure." Such people need to be taught how to recognize the positive around them. Successful people see the positive around them and gain energy from it.

Self-Discipline to Succeed

To create the attitude of successful people, it is not enough to be positive about your view of the world and to have a strong achievement motivation. There is the issue of maintaining the drive through the ups and downs of one's journey. To maintain the attitude for success, one has to develop a strong sense of self-discipline. The importance of this was supported in a research study by Angela Duckworth and Martin Seligman entitled "Self-Discipline Outdoes IQ in Predicting Academic Performance of Adolescents." They concluded that the lack success in school could not be blamed upon inadequate teachers, boring textbooks, or large class sizes, but rather, on the lack of self-discipline. In fact, self-discipline was more crucial to becoming successful in the academic world than intelligence. So if this is the case, then how is self-discipline developed?

One of the most exciting moments of a football game is before the kickoff, when the two teams are on their respective sidelines shouting, jumping up and down, beating on one another, generally "pumping" one another up to an emotional frenzy level to succeed. It might be nice if we could maintain that level of fire and desire as we face the challenges of daily life, but it just doesn't work out that way. Not a football team or any of us go through life that excited.

If we did so, we would either burn out quickly or be placed in a psychiatric hospital for uncontrollable mania. No, let's face it, some days we just don't feel very motivated. Some days we don't feel like running that lap, going to work, or even getting out of bed. Some days we just don't feel positive or motivated. And you know something, those football players who are so fired up before a game feel the same way sometime during the week. So how is it that come game time, they have the confidence and the skills to succeed? The answer is self-discipline, not emotion.

Self-discipline comes from the interaction of standards and routine. Standards define how something should be done, and routine gets it done. The football players are not filled with high emotional fire every day, but every day, they do what must be done to improve. When I used to run with patients as part of their therapy, we would jog or at least keep moving for thirty to forty-five minutes every day. Some days we might run farther or faster than others, but what was constant was that we did keep moving. In time, due to the consistency, they built the backlog of mileage so they were able to run farther and longer. In the morning, the alarm goes off and one person gets up and the other doesn't, yet both are very tired. The one who stays in bed thinks about the options; the one who gets up doesn't think, they *just do it*. In all of these examples, a standard has been set that is not debatable, and a routine is followed. The result is progress, and progress nurtures the positive attitude.

Throughout time, there have been standards of behavior established by man. Religion is based upon a belief and code of standards as to how man should behave. The Ten Commandments state how man should treat one another. The writings of Confucius give guidance as to how man should live his life. The teachings of Islam also lay out the ideal way of living one's life. Standards of what is the preferred and right way of treating one another are the bases of all of our laws. Criminal laws are basically antiabuse documents. We write and enforce laws to protect your right not to be abused by others. Such standards give us boundaries for our desires and guidance to what is fair and preferable. Successful people have clear standards under which they operate. When stressed or challenged, they turn to those standards for guidance and strength in making their decisions. The absence of standards leads to everything becoming a debate or a decision that can kill momentum. Be it a code of moral standards or a blueprint to becoming successful, having standards helps maintain the momentum of a positive and motivated person.

It is not uncommon for me to hear a person pledge their total self to achieving a goal or a way of living. They have reasonable, reachable goals and are motivated to pursue them, but maintaining this passion on a daily basis is the key. I remember talking with such an enthusiastic young man who wanted to stop gambling, stop doing drugs, and stop losing jobs. He pledged to change his life. To be successful at such a pledge, what you are pledging to has to be of paramount importance. You have to view that there is no alternative and that any other outcome is unacceptable. Such a commitment to a belief, decision, or goal is called a state of psychological primacy. If you would say that there is no amount of money that would get you to cut off your arm, you are saying that the retention of your arm is primary and priceless. There is no room for debate or consideration of an alternative. Such level of resolution to a principle guides and propels you forward and eliminates the struggle over what to do. The young man I mentioned decided that he would make a commitment to not gamble, use drugs again, or lose another job. To help make this happen, he also committed to daily activities and standards that reminded him of the positive direction he was taking in his life and the need for self-control. Being on time to work was not a debate, but a daily requirement. Working out and exercising daily became a constant in his routine. A significant portion of the money that he earned was to go directly into a bank account that he was not to touch until it reached a certain amount. Daily he would read a positive statement and reflect on its meaning. Socially, he would only surround himself with individuals who were positive and respectful of his desire to stay away from gambling and drug abuse. These were standards that helped guide and discipline him in his daily life on the way to a lifelong goal. While not everyone is faced with taking steps away from abuse, we all are faced with the challenge to take the path of self-improvement.

There is the story of Nido Qubein, who came to this country as a teenager not speaking the language, no contacts, and with only $50 in his pocket. He tells the story of his learning and using ten new words a day until he mastered the language. Because he believes that knowledge makes you successful, he spends one hour a day, every day, reading or listening to something new. Through such a routine, he developed the business savvy that has led him to starting a bank, sitting on the executive board of a Fortune 500 financial corporation with $115 billion in assets, being chairman of the board of the Great Harvest Bread Company, as well as serving on many other boards of successful corporations. He is a famous motivational speaker, a college president, and has been recognized for his philanthropic activities. The self-discipline that he applied to his routines became the fuel for his achievements and the foundation of his positive "I can do anything" attitude.

A positive, successful attitude can be learned. It is a reflection of the events and people around us. It grows in layers with each ensuing success. Its mortar is the daily self-discipline that we portray. And it all starts with a decision. A decision that there is no such thing as failure; there are only opportunities to learn and succeed. A decision that "failure is not an option."

Strategies to Develop the Winning Attitude

- *Positive is everywhere.* Carry a small notepad with you, and throughout the day, write down what you noticed is positive. It may be what someone says to you, it may be something that happens, it may be the weather; it doesn't matter what it is, just make a list. Keep track of your list and see if it gets longer each day. Unconsciously your list will probably get longer and, with it, your positive attitude.
- *Positives add up.* Some people find it is too intrusive to stop and write down what they see as positive. For such people, a "golf counter" would be indicated. A golf counter is a small device you can carry in your pocket, which, when a button is pushed or a wheel is turned, consecutive tabulation appears. Each day you keep track by the golf counter the number of positive events that were experienced that day. At the end of the day, you write down the total and reset the device for the next day. Hopefully, over time, the daily totals will increase, reflecting an increase in awareness and attitude.
- *Positive stories.* Just as the stories in this book can be inspirational, so can stories and movies elsewhere provide a sense of hope and drive. Stories about overcoming obstacles give us both a blueprint as to how to succeed and the belief that it can be done. Routine doses of positive pictures in our mind and on the screen can inoculate us against the negativity around us.
- *Positive music.* Music for many is a source of lifting the affect and the spirit. It is hard to be down or negative while being serenaded by an exciting rhythm and beat.
- *Preserve successes.* Keeping track of your successes provides you with reminders that you can be and have been a successful person. Some people make a list of successes; some put certificates, letters, and other symbols of their successes in a file that they can open and review when they need a boost. It is important to have reminders in your environment of successful events or challenges in the form of pictures, diplomas, or any other item that elicits positive memories and feelings. I was sitting in a psychiatrist's office one day and noticed that one whole wall was covered with certificates and diplomas. As I looked closer, along with his diplomas and licenses was a certificate for third-grade ball monitor. What a sign of health. Being the third-grade

ball monitor was a big success for him at that time, and today, to have it on the wall gives recognition to its importance in developing the successful person.

- *Self-Affirmations (exercise 5).* This exercise encourages you to make positive self-affirmations through the use of a self-monitoring log.
- *Reframing For Success (exercise 6).* The impact and ultimate interpretation of any situation depends upon how we look at what happened, how we framed it. A successful person is able to find the positives of a situation and use it to motivate themselves, as well as to make the best out of what worked out. This exercise helps you to reframe situations in order to focus your actions in a positive direction.
- *I Did It (exercise 7):* Big successes are built upon a series of smaller successes. This exercise encourages you to identify those moments when you could say, "I did it!" Such moments are the foundation from which self-confidence comes.
- *Dealing with Nonsuccesses (exercise 8):* There is no such thing as failure, only "nonsuccesses." How we interpret the "nonsuccessful" moments in our lives has much to do with how we will respond in the future. This exercise is designed to help you to identify the causes behind a nonsuccess so you can implement a successful moment in the future.
- *Creating Standards (exercise 9)* Start your own book of advice and standards by keeping a notebook in which you write down inspirational quotes or advice that you come across and has meaning to you.

A pessimist sees the difficulty in every opportunity;
An optimist sees the opportunity in every difficulty.
—*Winston Churchill*

How to Develop the Resources of Successful People

Behind an able man there are always
other able men.
—*Chinese Proverb*

Successful people know how to identify and utilize the resources necessary to succeed. The resources are the tools they use to do the job. There are many resources around us, but also inside us. Just as we may fly in a plane, it is the skill and knowledge of the pilot along with the plane that gets us to our destination. The presence of resources greatly impacts the creative solutions that emerge in the face of problems. You can only solve a problem with what you have, not with what you don't have. This is why it is important to not only know the resources available and how to use them, but also how to expand those resources.

External Resources

Resources are all around us. From spoons to the Internet to the sun above, resources are everywhere. In fact, there are so many resources around us that we often take them for granted and overlook their potential to help us. We don't see all of the possibilities and, therefore, sell short what can be accomplished. The great thinkers of time, such as Leonardo da Vinci, could take unrelated observations and resources and turn them into a new invention. Everything was in play, and the whole world was made up of pieces that could be reshuffled into new discoveries. For years each week on television, MacGyver would use bits of whatever he could find to create new ways escape from the clutches of his captors. It is not enough to identify resources; you have to also know how to use them for your benefit.

The first category or external resources are the objects we use. These comprise the tools we use to do the job. The hammers, forks, and cars of the world are resources that need no explanation because their use and value are defined by their very description. The more complex external resources that are nonhuman involves the sources where we get our information: books, television, radio, and Internet. Unlike a hammer, what you see when you use these resources is not always what you get. To use these resources effectively, you have to critically analyze what you are receiving. You have to separate fact from fiction, truth from lies, reality from propaganda. In school, training to be a psychologist, I learned to read a scientific study with a critical eye. I learned to challenge the methodology used in the experiment and how it might have impacted the results and the conclusions. That same critical analysis is needed as we are bombarded with information from everywhere. Information that may appear logical may actually be a very well constructed propaganda piece filled with a quarter of the facts and a sliver of the truth and a whole lot of bias and personal agenda. One safeguard against being manipulated is to check out what is being presented by consulting multiple sources. It is easy to confirm a statement that the circumference of the earth at the equator is 24,902 miles because it is easy to find more than one source to validate the information. Yet often times, opinion is presented as fact, making it even more crucial to validate what is fact and what is a sales pitch. Politicians are notorious for blending facts with opinions into a believable sales pitch. This is why it is important to use analysis and reason when cutting through the forest of information. Taking the time to research, discuss, and debate an issue will only build to a firmer foundation from which to decide the best course of action. In his book *The Assault on Reason*, the former vice president of the United States, Al Gore writes:

> *So the remedy for what ails our democracy is not simply better education (as important as that is) or civic education (as important as that can be), but the re-establishment of a genuine democratic discourse in which individuals can participate in a meaningful way—a conversation of democracy in which meritorious ideas and opinions from individuals do, in fact, evoke a meaningful response. (p. 254)*

It is the discourse between one another where lies the greatest resource of all, the resource of reason. It is the give and take of ideas where insight and creativity can grow. I have heard it said, "Beware of the man who keeps the consul of one." Isolating not only ourselves but also how we think opens us up to being manipulated by those who would pray on our narrow thinking. Reaching out to others and being open to new and different ideas only makes you freer to succeed.

Networking is a term heard often in motivation seminars and business classes. The need to develop a network of people that you can use or consult with to reach your goal is a fundamental given for any businessman, politician, or success-oriented person. The more people you know and the more meaningful your relationship, the more resources you have to be effective. Nido Qubein says there are three kinds of capital: financial capital, educational capital, and relationship capital. You have to work at building and maintaining your relationship capital as you would your financial. To do this, he reports calling four acquaintances a day just to see how they are doing. This keeps the relationship alive and more accessible when actual business needs to be done. You have a network now that you might want to take the time to identify and nurture. If you discover you need to expand your network, then identify who you should get to know and pursue meeting them. The old adage "you can never have too many friends" is true. Yet the nature of your friends can be more important than numbers.

Throughout time, the older, more experienced of the species have taught and guided the younger of the species. This has come to be called mentoring, coming from the Greek word *enduring*, meaning "the sustained relationship between a youth and an adult ... where the adult offers support, guidance, and assistance as the younger person goes through a difficult period, faces new challenges, or works to correct earlier problems" (www.ed.gov/pubs/OR/ConsumerGuides/mentor.

html). Having mentors throughout our lives is a valuable resource for knowledge and nurturing. In the biographies of successful people, you will find mentors that had some impact on the direction of their lives. The Carnegie Institute reports that there are three factors that are important in raising a healthy child in America today: (1) sense of safety and belonging in the home, school, and community; (2) three hours or more of organized activities weekly; and (3) three or more significant adults in their lives in addition to their parents. Where do these people come from? They come from relatives, teachers, coaches, scout leaders, clergy, and many other sources. These significant adults or mentors are needed not only in our youth, but throughout our lives. If you are about to embark upon pursuing your passion, find a mentor who has blazed a similar trail from whom you can learn and develop. The wisdom you gain from a mentor will surpass the knowledge you gain from books. A mentor is filled with practical knowledge and, if truly a mentor, is looking out for your best interests.

Finding a mentor depends upon what you are pursuing. If you are looking to start your own business, you may want to seek out retired businessmen in your area. Imparting information to the youth is often gratifying to a retired person and makes them feel that their knowledge is still valued. If you are in a training program or a school, the instructor is a logical potential mentor. There are governmental organizations such as SCORE Association (service corps of retired executives) and the Department of Defense that has a mentor-protégé program. Mentors are all around us; we just have to be open to them and be willing to nurture the relationship in return. The more respect shown to the mentor and the more excitement we display about what we are learning, the more the mentor will want to invest in us. While you are gaining concrete advice on how to proceed, the mentor needs to feel a connection to you to get the emotional gratification and validation that they need.

The importance of connecting is no clearer than it is when participating in a group setting. Within a group, you will find a gold mine of resources waiting to be discovered. In sports, business, education, and any situation where two or more people come together for a common purpose, you have a group. The other people in the group become a resource to not only help you accomplish a task, but also to help you develop the characteristics of successful people. You may have heard the claim that "sports builds character." It may be more accurate to say that sports provides lessons that help shape character. The importance of setting goals, working hard, maximizing teamwork, and facing the reality of outcomes are all crucial lessons in life. Yet sports alone are not the only group where lessons can be learned. Let's say you have a passion for saving the planet and putting an end to global warming. As an individual, you can educate yourself on the issue, change the lightbulbs in your home, and drive a more fuel-efficient car. If you were to join a group with the same passion you might learn more about the subject, meet other people with similar interests, observe and maybe participate in leadership positions, having a greater impact on the issue. Groups can have more impact than that of an individual. "*We* achieves more than *me*." Groups are a resource to educate you, to develop you, to help you reach your goal, and to provide you with more resources. Yet it is important to critically assess groups as you do an individual person. Groups have their own personality and can go through growing pains. The group's purpose may be confusing, agendas may be conflicting, and the group may be ineffective or dysfunctional. If you are faced with such a group, you have to decide if you need to adapt to it, change it, or escape from it. For example, let's say you are part of a group that wants to raise money for children's charities. Sounds like a good cause, but each week, the people in the group just talk and can't decide what to focus on. It appears that they are more interested in socializing and drinking than getting something done. If you are not interested in just partying and want to be part of something that will have an impact on children's lives, then you have a decision to make. You have to see how much you can adapt to the actions of the group or how much influence you can exert on changing the group, and if this is not enough, then you have to leave the group. If the group is not contributing to you reaching your goals, then you should leave. Groups, like people, go through growing pains. They may come together with a purpose, but as time goes by and the group grows, the purpose may get clouded or lost. When this happens, frustration and bickering in the group may grow, and the group members start to feed on one another rather than focus on the goal. It is important for the growth of the group that the participants be reminded of the mission and that there is an atmosphere of acceptance of diversity of ideas and people. It is from such diversity that creativity can emerge. As communication improves, trust is built and people feel more recognized and appreciated; the productivity of the group will grow. While groups may have their problems, they remain one of the most valuable resources in the development of a successful person.

Internal Resources

When taking stock of the resources at your disposal, you may want to start with yourself. Your skills, experiences, interests, values are all resources that you have to pull upon as you go along the road to success. You are a library of information just waiting to be categorized. It will pay to take the time to assess where you are at and what you have before seeking more. It's like when baking a cake and first checking the cupboards to see what ingredients you have before going to the store. You may save time, effort, and money.

The first resource inventory for you to take involves your values. What is it that you value and how do your values affect your actions. We talked about this previously when we explored finding your passion. It is important to know what you value because it is from your values that much of your personal strength comes. What you value comes through in your dealings with others and the decisions you make. Knowing what you hold in highest esteem will guide you in what you will not do as much what you will do. When an individual is clearly aware of what they value, they are less apt to be manipulated or surprised by conflicting beliefs. Finding where your values lie is the composite of approaches. You can review with yourself or with the help of others how you handled different situations and what was important to you as reflected in the action you took. Did you speak up when you thought the boss was wrong, or did you choose to live and let live? Neither action is right or wrong; it is just an expression of what you value. Another way to see the relationship between your values is to complete value clarification inventories or exercises. These activities are designed to make you think and question the significance of one of your values over another value. After completing the identification of your values, you can next ask the important question: "Am I living my life consistent with my values?"

While you are looking within, make a list of all of the skills you have. During the course of our life, we accumulate the mastery of different tasks in school, at work, and in daily life, which, today, we may have lost touch with or overlooked. Review the duties of the jobs you have held and note all the specific and general skills you obtained. Maybe you worked in a gas station. You gained the specific skill of changing a tire, but you also gained experience at working with the public. While some specific skills may not be transferable between jobs, there are others that are fundamental to a vast majority of job opportunities. A woman who has spent years raising children might believe that she has no marketable skills, but this is just not true. She knows how to manage and organize a household, getting tasks completed, getting people to where they need to be on time, and handling a budget. Now, don't you think that there are many employers looking for people with this skill set? Yet we often sell short what we know in favor of longing for what we don't know. Yes, such a review of skills will help identify what we don't know and what training or experience we need to obtain. But it may also serve to let us see that we are not as far from getting the skills we need than was first thought.

Related to value clarification and skills clarification is interest clarification. What we are interested in is a resource to motivate and direct us. Our interests grow in the same garden as our values, abilities, and personality. Research has shown that those who are attracted to and enjoy certain occupations also have similar values, personalities, and interests. In addition to personal observation, another way to identify your interests is to complete one of the many interest inventories that are often used in job search counseling. These inventories are standardized on responses given by individuals who are happily pursuing a particular occupation. Your responses to the questions are then compared to the standardized group to determine which occupations you are most apt to enjoy.

Another internal resource is your personal fund of general knowledge. This is the accumulation of all that you have learned from study and experience. In assessing the extent of your general fund of knowledge, identifying your values, skills, and interests is part of the process. Another part is discovering how much information in your brain have you stored and can retrieve at will. Knowledge doesn't come only in those areas where we have high interest, it comes from unrelated areas as well. Expanding one's knowledge base allows the cross-referencing of ideas and increased confidence in a variety of situations. The acquisition of general knowledge does not have to stop when we graduate from school. We can be lifelong learners like Franklin, Edison, or Da Vinci if only open to be so. Reading a daily newspaper or weekly magazines such as *Time* or *Newsweek* or watching the nightly news can expand our awareness of the world beyond our own into disciplines we rarely have contact. Successful people have a broad range of interests, which constantly stimulate a thirst to drink more from the cup of knowledge.

Communication and people skills are two somewhat related skills that have a significant impact on becoming successful. Being skilled at communicating allows us to be better understood and to avoid many conflicts. I have sat for years hearing couples argue about what they want from their marriage and what the other one isn't giving to them, only to note that they are saying and wanting the same thing. They just don't hear what is being said. The road to good communication starts with good listening. Being a good listener means you take everything in that is being said as opposed to thinking about what you are going to say next. Most arguments are the result of not listening and then responding to what you thought was said, clouded by your own frustration. Maintaining eye contact and feeding back what you heard reassures the speaker that they are being listened to. This also communicates that you respect the other person and what they are saying is important to you. You may disagree with the other person, but at least they feel understood. While listening is crucial to understanding, being able to express yourself in a way that can be understood is equally important. By improving your vocabulary, grammar, and written skills, you not only will be better understood, but you will also sound more knowledgeable and confident.

Not everyone will become a public speaker or a famous writer, but being able to state your point of view clearly and effectively allows others to join you in your vision for the future. Selling your idea to others begins with you selling yourself on the value of the resource of good communication.

An often-abused resource that may be viewed more as a value or philosophy than a resource is the showing of respect for others. We all want to be respected for who we are and what we do. We like the reinforcement that comes from the attention of others because it validates our identity and self-worth. Those who take the time to give attention to others become valuable people who are sought out and listened to more, thus getting back the recognition they send. It may be as little as a nod of acknowledgement or making eye contact, but what it communicates can speak volumes. Listening is giving attention and showing respect. Using good manners in how and what you say is a show of respect. Seeing diversity and difference as providing beauty to our landscape and not a threat is showing respect. The displaying of respect is an attitude and a behavior. By having the attitude that leads to showing respect to others, you will receive respect in return, which will validate your belief in the power of respect.

For the successful person, the whole world is a resource to be used to reach their goals. Yet there are those who see using some resources as limiting their freedom and independence. They view a mentor as someone to tell them when they are wrong or what won't work. They are resistant to prescribed medications, citing they don't like how they feel about it even though it is necessary for their health, behavior control, or emotions. Such people's resistance to using whatever resources necessary to be successful are being resistant to being successful. Successful people see everything and everybody as a potential resource and are willing to use whatever is available, while never being deterred by what is not present. When needing a tool, they seek it out or learn to work around it. Money is a great resource, but when not available, finding the resources to raise money or to do the project with less money is equally important. Successful people know that resources are the tools necessary to build the house of success.

Strategies to Identify Winning Resources

- *Know Your Skills (exercise 10)*. Knowing your areas of strength and weaknesses is valuable information in designing your road to success. In this exercise, you are to rate yourself on a list of skills and in so doing, learn more about yourself personal resources.

- *Identifying Resources (exercise 11).* It is one thing to be able to identify the resources you need to achieve a goal, but it is another to find a way to succeed with the resources you have. This exercise is designed to challenge your thinking about identifying and utilizing resources.
- *Identifying Human Resources (exercise 12).* The greatest resources around us are the people we know, yet rarely do we stop to identify the extent that they are a resource. This exercise is designed to help you to identify the many talents, knowledge, contacts, and personal attributes of the people around you that could be taped as a resource for you.

> *One of the secrets of life is to make*
> *stepping stones out of the stumbling*
> *blocks.*
>
> —*Ken Blanchard*

How to Make the Decisions of Successful People

> *Everything can be taken from a man but . . .*
> *the last of the human freedoms—to choose*
> *one's attitude in any given set of circumstances,*
> *to choose one's own way.*
>
> —*Victor Frankl*

The freedom to choose is God-given and cannot be taken away from us even if our options are not pretty. Recognizing that we are the keepers of that freedom makes us responsible to use it wisely. The ability to make well thought-out decisions is the source of our power and provides the direction to each step we take. Successful people recognize their power to make decisions and use it wisely in charting the course they will take.

True independence comes when we realize that we make all of the decisions in our life. Oh, you can say, "My boss told me to do it. I had no choice." But in reality, you did have a choice. You could have decided to not do what your boss said and suffer the possible consequences of being fired. Since you wanted to keep your job, you *decided* to comply. The key is that you decided. This can be a pressure for some people because they don't want the responsibility of deciding. They would rather remain a victim to the decisions of others. So the initial factor in making good decisions is a willingness to be in control of your life. That is, in fact, the first good decision you will make.

This doesn't mean that you become extremely bossy and decide to be in control of everything around you. You may decide to defer the decision making in particular situations because another person is more knowledgeable or skilled than you. As long as you recognize that you made that decision you will not become a victim of what was decided. Successful people are not victims, but rather, take charge of their lives and decide the course they will take.

A willingness to make your own decisions and how to make those decisions are two different things. Years ago, while watching some students arguing on the playground, it hit me that they looked like a couple of long horned sheep banging their heads together. They could have been arguing whether the ball was fair of foul or whose turn it was; it didn't matter. What was happening was that each of them was escalating into a physical fight without any attempt to solve the conflict fairly and logically. I then noticed another student watching who then stepped in and offered a solution, which ended the conflict, and the game was able to be continued. The image of two rams butting heads with a third one watching led to a method of decision making called RAM, which stands for *relax, analyze,* and *move.* I had a drawing made portraying the basic message to kids of "do you want to be two rams butting heads or the third one using your head for thinking?"

RELAX - ANALYZE - MOVE

How to make decisions really does come down to RAM . . . relax, analyze, and move.

Relax

It is widely recognized in the world of sports that if you are tense, your muscles will not respond as quickly, and you will not assess a situation as clearly. An athlete wants to have adrenaline flowing to provide the drive, but be relaxed enough to allow their natural and trained instincts to take over. That same principle applies to all situations in life. Whenever we are stressed, our thought processes are focused on the threat and less so on exploring the options for a solution. The distraction that stress creates harms our being creative and blocks the retrieval of information that we know might help us. Ask any student who has test anxiety, and they will tell you how they have difficulty remembering what they know. When confronted with a decision, step back and relax enough to get centered and in control. If it is a threatening situation, like being confronted by a snarling boss, take a deep breath, relaxing your body as much as you can. This will allow you an opportunity to better listen and process what is being said before responding.

The importance of relaxing applies not only to high-energy situations, but rather, to all situations where problem solving and creativity are involved. Thomas Edison is the example I used before in regard to getting in touch with your passion, and the same story applies to problem solving as well. It has been reported that Thomas Edison, the great inventor, frequently was found dozing off while working on one of his inventions and then waking up with the solution of what he was working on. Edison's catnaps were probably a way that allowed his unconscious to work on the problem uninterrupted by other events. When he awoke, he could see the situation he was working on in another way, and the solution became clear. There are other ways to relax and clear your mind other than taking catnaps. I have found in the course of writing this book that I organized my thoughts better while walking or jogging. Music can serve as mantra to both relax and inspire. There are those who swear by the powers of a long bubble bath or massage to revitalize their thinking. Whatever approach you apply to relax, taking time to focus on the many aspects of a situation, unobstructed by a tirade of emotions, will lead to clearer and more successful solutions.

Analyze

The making of decisions requires analyzing the facts involved and the possible outcomes of one's decision in the light of the chosen criteria for success. This first requires a desire to see all aspects of a situation, the good and bad. Some people prefer to see only one side of a problem and seek out only the information that supports their point of view. Such as someone who has one political view listening to or reading only information that comes from like-minded people. Such a person has decided to have their point of view confirmed rather than deciding to explore what are all the facts of a situation. To make good informed decisions, all aspects of a situation have to be explored. When this is done, you will be better able to determine what are the advantages and disadvantages of the possible actions you may take. Successful people consistently make decisions that are to their advantage. Being involved in drugs or substance abuse is clearly to one's disadvantage. Making decisions that avoid self-harm are clearly to one's advantage. But not all decisions are so clear. Many need a systematic process of analysis for the best options to emerge. Before buying a new car, a successful person might research the mileage and the repair records of two cars. The facts may make it clear which would be a better investment. But here is where the criteria for a decision becomes a factor. The person buying the car may decide that the make or appearance of the car is more important than the economic factors. So while one person may decide to buy the big-engine, gas-using sports car, another person chooses the economical hybrid sedan; and both people are successful. They are successful because they satisfied their criteria for success.

Many times, what needs to be analyzed is not so much what lies before us but rather what occurred in the past. It has been said that "history will repeat itself." If we do not want to repeat the errors of the past, then we need to understand what led to today's decision. While working with conduct disordered kids, I came across a lesson called the ABCs of conflict situations in a book entitled *Aggression Replacement Training*. I tweaked the lesson into the ABCD of problem solving. *A* stands for *activating event*, which would be anything that would be a stimulus that you respond to, such as a sunset, a car accident, or something someone has said. *B* stands for *behavior*, which includes your thoughts, feelings, and actions in response to the activating event. *C* stands for the *consequences*, which resulted from the behavior you took. And *D* stands for the need to *decide* what you have to do next or what you have to do differently next time. As an example, let's say the activating event for a student is getting a poor grade on a test. The student's behavior is to blow up at the teacher when the test is returned. The consequence of such behavior leads to the student being sent to office and suspended for a few days for disrespect to a teacher. As a result of what happened, the student may want to analyze this course of events to determine what could be done differently if the same activating event occurred. From such analysis, hopefully the student will learn to avoid such unproductive behaviors and decide to pursue a more successful course of action. Analyzing our past is important in order to learn more about ourselves and to learn from our mistakes and successes.

Move

Move means to decide upon which course of action you will take after you have analyzed the history, factors, and consequences of the situation or problem that is confronting you. Some decisions are very difficult to make, but knowledge sheds light on an issue, which adds clarity to which way to move. The more facts or information one has, the more evident does the next course of action become. The facts actually make the decision for you. My wife tells the story of when she was a nurse in an emergency room, assisting an intern with a patient, when suddenly, the patient stopped breathing and blew an aortic aneurysm, going into cardiac arrest. The intern started to apply compressions to the patient's chest as other personnel and surgeons came running into the room. The attending ER doctor, upon entering, assessed the situation in a split second, and as the intern raised his hands, going back from the compression, the senior doctor with one swipe of his scalpel opened the chest of the patient in order to apply direct heart massage. The patient was stabilized enough to be rushed to surgery. What might look like split-second decision making was actually a split-second assessment making based upon years of training and experience that resulted in only one possible course of action.

Most of us are not faced with life or death decisions, but we are faced with decisions that might change the course of our life or that of others. It is important then that we collect all the information available and explore every option before we decide. Yet in any given situation, we do not decide only once; we repeatedly decide to continue what we are doing or to stop what we are doing and alter our course of action. As new information comes into us, it is important to add it to our decision-making process and determine if what we are doing is working or if we should make a new decision. Abraham Lincoln was once confronted on going back on what he said he would do. Today in politics, he would be accused of "flip-flopping." Lincoln responded to such criticism by saying that he hadn't failed to live up to what he had said; he just changed his mind due to new information. The ability to be flexible is important in decision making. As you learn from what you are doing and more information comes in, a refinement of the decision and your actions should be made. The constant adjusting and adapting to a situation is what successful people do willingly and naturally.

Strategies for Making Winning Decisions

- *Analyzing Decisions (exercise 13).* One of the simplest ways of determining which decision you should make is to divide a piece of paper in half, labeling one side *Advantages* and the other *Disadvantages.* The analyzing the pros and cons exercise provides you with various ways of analyzing what is on your list to help you come to a decision.

- *Decision Tree (exercise 14).* A *decision tree* can be a great way to visualize the relationship between problem, possible solutions, and consequences. You may want to actually draw a tree with a trunk, limbs, and leaves. On the trunk, you write the problem. On the limbs, you write all of the possible choices to solve the problem, and from leaves on the limb, you write all the possible consequences of that option. For example, a child may be faced with the dilemma of staying home and doing his homework or going to the game with his friend. On the trunk is the problem: doing homework versus going to the game. On one limb, you could write, "go to the game" with the leaves stating "see game," "be with friends," "fail assignment." On another limb, you could write, "Stay home and do homework," with the leaves stating, "pass the assignment," "friends be mad at me," "miss the game." On a third limb, you may write, "do the homework at the game," with leaves stating "finish homework," "lose homework," "wouldn't get it done," A fourth limb might read "get answers to homework from a peer," with the leaves having "finish homework and pass," "get caught for cheating," and "not learn the material." After completing your tree, you can sit back and see the options and the possible outcomes of your choices. If drawing a tree is not your thing, you can use boxes leading out from the problem, followed by more boxes listing possible outcomes coming out from the possible options. Either method is designed to help you see the linear relationship to your decision.

- *Decision Making: Plus-Minus Implications (exercise 15).* A variation of listing the advantages/disadvantages and the decision tree methods is the plus-minus-implications approach. In this method, you would write across the top of your paper "Plus," "Minus," and "Implications." Under "Plus," you would write the positive results of your taking the action. Under the "Minus," you list the negative effects. Under "Implications," you write the possible outcomes both positive and negative. You can assign point values to each of the items listed, giving positive points to the plus column, negative points to each item in the minus column, and positive or negative points to the implications.

- *ABCD of Problem Solving (exercise 16).* Understanding what leads up to a decision you must make is important in making that decision. This exercise guides you in breaking down a problem or situation into the components of activating event, behavior, and consequences before you decide what is your next step or what to do differently next time.

- *ACE Your Problems (exercise 17):* All problems, no matter how complex, have only three possible solutions. You can "adapt or adjust" to the situation, you can "change" the situation, or you can "escape" the situation. Adapt, change, or escape—ACE. This exercise guides you in analyzing your options in terms of ACE.

> *If one does not know to which port is sailing,*
> *no wind is favorable.*
>
> —*Seneca*

How to Design the Schemes of Successful People

> *Give me a stock clerk with a goal and I'll give you*
> *a man who will make history. Give me a man with no*
> *goals and I'll give you a stock clerk.*
>
> —*J. C. Penney*

Schemes are the roadmaps of our life, and our goals are the destinations we seek. Without goals and how we plan to achieve them, we are nothing more than seaweed drifting at the mercy of the currents and winds around us. Our goals are the stars that give us direction, and our scheme is the ship we build to take us there. Many will recite their goals, but only the successful can describe their plan to get there.

The designing of a successful scheme starts with proper goal setting and visualization as described in the opening section of this book. Remember, a good goal has to be definable, achievable, desirable, measurable, and controllable. Goals that do not pass the test of these five ingredients only increase the likelihood of failure. Next, you have to visualize the goal as vividly as you can. The more you can see the goal, the clearer will you see what has to be done to reach it. Yet even more important, being able to clearly visualize succeeding at your goal will serve as a magnet to pull and inspire your drive toward it. These are the two basic fundamentals of designing a successful scheme; now let us look closer at how to build on these fundamentals.

You may have heard people say, "I have goals, they are in my head." I'm glad that these people have goals, but our minds are constantly flowing and changing direction as we take in new information. This barrage of information can easily lead to distractions, disorganization, and even forgetting. By writing down the goal, it becomes constant, which is much better than our memory. Written goals clarify thinking, concretize our direction, and remind us of our commitment. Goals that are out of sight will be out of mind. You may also hear, "Ya, I know I need to write down my goals, but it takes too long." It takes too long! How much time are you spending going in circles? Any successful athlete or team will tell you that their success does not solely depend upon their performance on the day contested, but rather upon the preparation leading up to that day. I have heard it said, "Success is when preparation meets opportunity." The time you spend writing down and refining your goals is the preparation that is needed to reach the goals. Your performance will only be enhanced by the time you invest in developing your goal and scheme. Some may reply that you can do too much scheming, which will lead to "paralysis by analysis," and what you need to do is to just go for it. It is true that you can get lost in analyzing a situation to the point that you don't move, yet jumping into something without fully analyzing it could lead to a waste of your time going in unproductive directions. Learn to work smart. Learn to take the time to write down your goals and scheme.

Once you have established your primary goals, the next task is to identify what steps are required to reach that goal. The more detailed the steps, the clearer will be your vision of your journey to the goal and the more motivated you will become to reach the goal. Goals that are not bridged with intermediate goals may look too overwhelming and retard progress. Think of each identified step as a goal, and make note of the accomplishment when it is achieved. For example, the goal may be to get an A on a history final test at the end of the semester. This is definable, achievable, desirable, measurable, and controllable (assuming that you are not in a class beyond your skill level and that the teacher will give an A to anyone). To get that A, there are a list of steps or subgoals that can be made. They may include but are not limited to the following: (1) attend all classes, (2) take notes in all classes, (3) read all assigned material, (4) complete all assignments, (5) ask for assistance when having difficulty understanding any material, (6) review and study material a minimum of thirty minutes a night, (7) review and rehearse material prior to the test, (8) get sufficient sleep prior to the test, and (9) remain calm and focused during the test. Going a little further, each of these subgoals can be defined and broken down into measurable terms so that you know when you have achieved them. By laying it out in this manner, you have identified your scheme for achieving an A on the history final.

For goals that involve covering territory that is more uncharted than earning a grade in a class, you need to break down your journey by establishing the *what* and *how* of that journey. Being able to answer the following questions will help you in creating the roadmap to your goal:

- Where are we going, and how do we know when we get there?
- What are the things that will keep us from where we are going, and how do we eliminate them?
- What are the major milestones along the way to where we are going?
- What are the *things* that must be done to get to each milestone?
- Of what specific tasks are the *things* composed?
- What are the possible ways of getting the *things* done?

Once you can answer these questions, the topography and challenges of your journey becomes clearer. What is left is to line the resulting minigoals up and reach them one at a time.

While it is important to set a goal and be dedicated to work hard to achieve it, it is even more important learn to work smart. This means being realistic and flexible when the path to a goal has an obstacle. Encountering obstacles to goals is part of the process. How you adapt and adjust to the challenges presented by the obstacle may very well determine if the goal is ever achieved. When faced with a boulder in the middle of the road, do you change your coarse and go around it or spend your time trying to blast through it? The road to success is not always a straight line, and true success may actually hinge on the ability to adapt. A successful hitter in baseball is the one who is able to adjust to what the pitcher is throwing. A pilot when he encounters a storm alters his altitude and air speed to reach his destination. A person with health problems makes the changes in their diet and life habits to stay alive. It has been said that the key to successful mental health is the ability to adapt to what is presented to us as opposed to stubbornly maintaining an unsuccessful behavior. I have also heard it said that the definition of stupidity is to attempt repeatedly that which does not work, expecting a different result. Intelligence is knowing when to change course to achieve success. Changing course may also include being alert to refining the steps to the goal in order to accomplish more in less time, with a fraction of the effort. This requires regular review of the scheme and the honest assessment of the progress toward the goal. If something is not working, change it.

Strategies for Making a Winning Scheme:

- *Making a Winning Goal (exercise 18).* A winning goal is a goal that is built for success. Too often, goals are not properly constructed, and they are doomed to fail before you get started. For a goal to have the chance to be successful, it has to be definable, achievable, desirable, measurable, and controllable. This exercise is designed to help you to identify these five elements and formulate them in to a winning goal.

161

- *Analyzing Your Goal (exercise 19).* Once you have identified a goal, this exercise is designed to help you in identifying what lies ahead on the road to achieving your goal.
- *Webbing a Goal (exercise 20).* A goal is really a series of minigoals that must be reached to finally achieve the primary goal. This exercise is a brainstorming activity that helps in breaking down and visualizing the steps required to reach a goal.
- *Getting It Done (exercise 21).* Having a goal is the first step, but you will be standing in place if you don't devise a plan for getting it done. This exercise provides another method for breaking down a goal into smaller goals or steps that will need to be achieved in order to achieve the primary goal.
- *Time Management (exercise 22).* Good intentions are often destroyed by poor execusion. The poor use of your time can lead to not only wasted time, but also missed opportunities and success. Good time management does not mean working harder, but rather working smarter. To do this you have to know the following: (1) what has to get done, (2) what is important, (3) how much time you have, and (4) how motivating is the task. It is the integration of these factors that makes for good time management. This exercise helps you analyze the tasks you have to perform so you can arrange your time in the most effect and productive way.

> *You got to be careful if you don't know where*
> *you're going, because you might not get there.*
> —*Yogi Berra*

All That Is Left Is to "Just Do It"

> *If hard work is the key to success, most people*
> *would rather pick the lock.*
> —*Claude McDonald*

Knowing how to play the cards you were dealt to be successful is actually only half of the issue. What is left is actually playing the cards. It takes the right commitment, attitude, resources, decision making, and scheme to be successful, but it also takes effort. We have all heard people say, "I could have done this" or "I could have been that," but you aren't *this* or *that* because you didn't *do it*. Success is measured by what you have accomplished, not by what you have dreamed of or desired. We all want to be successful, but only those who do what it takes become successful.

> *Even if you are on the right track,*
> *You'll get run over if you just sit there.*
> —*Will Rogers*

The road map to success may now be clear, but it takes you to provide the gas to get there. Success takes hard work and sacrifice, two things that not everyone is willing to do. Success does not come easy, but the more you take the steps toward success, the easier it becomes. You start to live your life in the ways of successful people. Not afraid of working hard, but rather, energized by doing. Being able to set priorities and willing to make sacrifices to achieve them. Preferring to play your own cards rather than watching the game from the sideline. It is time to sit at the card game of life and start playing if you are ever going to start achieving your quest to be successful.

> *Procrastination is opportunity's natural assassin.*
> —*Victor Kiam*

Playing CARDS with Others

Coming together is a beginning.
Keeping together is progress.
Working together is success.

—*Henry Ford Sr.*

At the risk of sounding like some snake oil salesman who claims their product can cure anything that ails you, CARDS can be applied to more than serving as ingredients of success for an individual. The same principles that apply to an individual's success can also guide a business, a nation, and a worldwide issue to success. Like an individual, a group can become committed to a goal, develop within the group the attitude needed to succeed, identify and pull together the resources needed, collaborate in making the most productive decisions, and design a scheme to follow to reach success. A group is a collection of individual talents, skills, dreams, experiences, and successes that when put into a unified whole, can propel everyone to new heights and greater feats. The strength and impact of one individual can be multiplied by the size of the group when committed to a common goal. Analyzing the group process in terms of CARDS can only help in reaching the group's goal.

In business, we hear a lot about the importance of a business plan. A detailed analysis of how the product will go from concept to consumption. How will the product be produced, marketed, and sold? The goal of such plan is to determine the feasibility of the project, how to minimize the downsides and surprises while maximizing the upside and success. Companies who have clear and complete business plans make few mistakes and are confident in their chances of success. In fact, they often analyze the situation so completely that they take chance out of the equation, leaving only predictable success. CARDS provides a framework for a successful business plan.

To understand further how to apply CARDS to a business, consider this hypothetical example. Let's say you own the "I Am Great" ice cream company, we'll call it IAG for short. IAG executives are worried about a drop in sales and have determine they need a new product. Their research has shown that there is an increased awareness on the part of the general public as to what is healthier to eat. People still want to eat ice cream, but the effects it has on their health have resulted in a reduction of consumption. In other words, the desire to eat ice cream is still there, but the right product is not. IAG has to come up with a satisfying ice cream that also satisfies the customer's desire for greater health. The first step for IAG is to determine if there is enough of a level of *commitment* to the new product not only on the part of the customer, but also within the organization. IAG had always been dedicated to making ice cream the *old-fashioned way*. This will require a new way of thinking within the company and the marketing department. Could IAG generate the positive *attitude* that would lead to the dedication necessary to develop, produce, and market a new and different product? There needed to be an assessment of their existing and nonexisting *resources*. Could their labs create a new low-fat ice cream? Could they dedicate and retool a portion of their existing plants for the new product, and how much would this cost? How should they market the new product? All of these questions needed to be considered and analyzed so that good *decisions* could be made. Once all of this had been accomplished, IAG needed to make a *scheme* that would lay out the path from conception to production to delivery to marketing to consumption. For their new ice cream to be a money maker, it would take total commitment, the right attitude, the necessary resources, good decision making, and a detailed scheme. If IAG played their cards right, sales should go up, and their company profits should rise.

While in one sense, every group project is about selling something much like a business product, there are some differences in the obstacles that need to be overcome. Let's say a school is considering implementing a new curriculum of their own design. CARDS can still be applied in approaching this task, but the emphasis on the aspects of commitment and attitude may be more crucial than it is in the business setting. In the business setting, the commitment issue is often settled by the boss saying that this is what I want to happen. The need to please the boss translated into a paycheck seals the commitment question and goes a long way at promoting the attitude level. But with a group of individuals whose purpose in participating is abstract and individualized in nature, the importance of establishing a commitment to a common purpose is much more difficult. Each individual may have their own agenda and want to be heard in the shaping of the group's purpose. It is important that everyone is listened to and their position is considered so they can make a commitment to the task at hand.

This process of listening and considering everyone's ideas will increase a sense of investment and identification with the project and will contribute much to the attitude with which the task will be approached. Once the mission statement of the group has been established, an analysis of the resources of the group and school should be made. Some ideas may be great to have implemented, but there aren't the resources financially or time wise to do so. A careful accounting of the resources will narrow down the decisions that need to be made. Again, decision making in a "volunteer" group is much different than that found in business. In business, there is a chain of command, and there is always someone who will make the ultimate decision. With a volunteer group, the process of decision making isn't so black-and-white. Whenever there are not concrete, disputable facts to use in the decision making, there will be room for debate. There are biases, feelings, and opinions to consider in analyzing and making decisions. Although time consuming, this is not bad because from a melting pot of open discussion can come clarity, increased commitment, and accuracy in the decision reached. From these decisions, the scheme to implement the task, or in this case the curriculum, can be developed and followed.

The approach suggested by CARDS can be taken to resolve any problem no matter the size. I know; feelings of grandiosity on my part are setting in again. "One solution could not fit all problems," you say. But maybe it is the nature and size of a problem that is complex and not the method to use to reach a successful resolution of the problem. Maybe the riddle of poverty, discrimination, war, and global warming could be solved if only we learned how to play our CARDS.

Let's consider global warming. The term is used to identify the crisis the planet is facing as our climate patterns change and natural resources are eradicated. For years, scientists have studied the process and made warnings of potential disasters ahead, but few listened. Sure, Jimmy Carter, during his presidency, promoted the value of conservation, but the level of commitment for significant change to take place did not happen, and the solar energy cells he had put on the White House were removed by the next president. Al Gore spoke and wrote about his concerns about global warming while vice president, but still, few listened, and nothing of significance was done. Once out of office, Gore's individual commitment to the cause led him to personally give PowerPoint presentations on the subject to small groups across the county. The numbers of believers grew, and grew even more with his documentary, *An Inconvenient Truth*. As the weather patterns became more unpredictable and destructive, more people started to listen to what he and others were saying about saving our planet. The movement grew, resulting in a shift from disbelief that it was happening to what should we do about it. The commitment and attitude phase had started but would need to be reaffirmed along the way. As with the principles behind motivation described earlier, the world needs to be shown what can be done and that achieving a reversal of the greenhouse effect is possible for the commitment of the individual to grow and success achieved. The global warming movement is identifying the resources needed and available to make a change. Decisions will need to be made on an individual, national, and worldwide level as to given the resources at hand, what decisions need to be made, and what schemes need to be followed in order to save the planet. Today, individuals may be willing to change the type of lightbulb they use, but not the fuel in their car. As the availability and feasibility of alternative resources for energy increase, the motivation and level of commitment will change. Today, the challenge is in the details needed to produce change, and the method to break down those details lies within the CARDS.

A systematic method such as CARDS may have no impact upon the cards a group, nation, or world are dealt, but it can do much in determining how to best play those cards and thus win the card game of life.

Teaching CARDS in the Classroom

The dream begins with a teacher who believes in you,
who tugs and pushes and leads you to the next plateau,
sometimes poking you with a sharp stick called "truth."
                                                    —*Dan Rather*

Since being successful can be taught, a natural place to plant the seeds of success is to apply the concept of CARDS in the classroom. As more and more educators look to include character education and school-to-career curriculum in the classroom, the need for methods to easily integrate such curriculum into an already overflowing plate of academic expectations becomes paramount. For any self-improvement curriculum to be successful, it has to be taught and then reinforced repeatedly over time. If the applications of what is being taught can be seen to apply throughout the day and cross subjects, the strength of the lesson increases. CARDS can be and has been taught in an English course, but the concepts can apply to a history, study skills, or career-planning course just as well. The vocabulary of CARDS and the methods of analyzing a situation can be applied schoolwide, which will reinforce the ingredients for success even more. One advantage of CARDS in response to the curriculum demands of teachers is that the basic lesson of CARDS is short and easily taught. The activities to reinforce the lesson can be integrated into existing reading, writing, or self-improvement lessons.

The activities that can be generated from CARDS are limited only to the time, creativity, and motivation of the instructor. Many of the activities listed in the appendix and below have been used in a high school classroom. They would also be appropriate with some modifications for younger students. After reading the list, you may think of other ways to integrate CARDS into your classroom curriculum.

Strategies for Teaching CARDS

- *Find It in the CARDS (exercise 23).* After teaching the principles of CARDS, have the students read a story from the Journeys to Success section of this book and have them answer the following questions:

  o What was the primary *commitment* or passion of the person?
  o What are examples of the *attitude* that contributed to them being successful?
  o What *resources* contributed to the person's success?
  o What *decisions* did the person make that led to their success?
  o What was the *scheme* the person followed to become successful?

- Have the student read a biography of a famous person and analyze their story in the terms outlined above or using the Find it in the CARDS worksheet.
- Have the student interview a person they admire, such as a parent, friend or acquaintance, utilizing the questions listed above to structure the interview.
- Have the student watch a movie in which the main character was successful and produce an analysis of the character and movie in the above terms.

  o Analyze an event in history utilizing CARDS. For example, you could break down the role of the United States in World War II by exploring such questions as (1) What contributed to changing the U.S. commitment to entering into the war? (2) What attitudes, self-discipline, or sacrifices contributed to ultimate success? (3) What resources were utilized and developed to become victorious? (4) What decisions were made that led to success? (5) What was the scheme that led to victory?

- *Winning with CARDS in the Classroom (exercise 24).* At the start of a class, have the students write how they will approach the class in terms of CARDS. What are they committed to as a grade? What attitude and systems of self-discipline will they need to succeed in the class? What resources will they use to get the grade they desire in the class? What decisions will they have to make in regards to how they spend their time and what they can't do if they are to be successful? What scheme or routine will they develop to be successful in the class?

- *Thirty Years from Now (exercise 25).* Have the student imagine that it is thirty years from today, and they are reflecting upon the successful life they have enjoyed. They are to write the story of their own journey to success in the manner as those written in this book. They are to incorporate the five ingredients that make up CARDS. The exercise sheet is designed to provide a guide for the students.

- *Life's Dilemmas (exercise 26).* The decisions one makes in their lives are not always black-and-white. It is when values come in conflict that the true definition and beliefs of a person become evident. This exercise provides challenging everyday conflicts, which the student must analyze and decide what to do. This exercise can be used as a writing assignment or for a classroom discussion.

> *Tell me and I'll forget, show me and I may remember,*
> *involve me and I'll understand.*
>
> —*Chinese Proverb*

The Final CARDS

I'll let go of what I was,
accept myself for what I am,
and become who I was meant to be.

—Unknown

When I started my journey to write this book about ten years ago, my desire was to learn more about what it takes to be successful. During the course of this journey, I have seen that successful people have a commitment to something or someone that is the source of their passion and direction in life. I discovered that successful people share an attitude and perspective on life that does not accept the concept of failure. To them, "failure is not an option," leaving only twists and turns to be navigated on their road to success. I have come to appreciate the role that the resources around and within us play in becoming successful. I have had confirmed to me the importance of sound decision making, and that true power comes from the realization that while you may not be in control of your choices, you are always in control of your decisions. And I have come to appreciate the importance of a scheme that establishes one's goals and charts the course to reach those goals. I have seen these factors in becoming successful exhibited in a wide variety of people and occupations, which begs the conclusion that success is universally attainable and is not about the end, but rather, the process toward the end.

When I ask students or patients to define for me "What is success?" I get as many answers as there are people. Eventually, a consensus is arrived at that success is different for everyone. In other words, the definition of success is a very personal thing and involves defining the person more than defining an outcome. About six months before finishing this book, I reflected upon the basic "What is success" question of this book and the very personal nature of the response.

As I tried to resolve the issue of the unhappy rich man and the satisfied poor man, it hit me that there was in fact one true definition of success. I started to see that while there may be many different kinds of success, there was also one common element that is success. This element transcends riches or fame or surmounting great challenges. This element is often difficult to recognize yet so very simplistic in its uttering. This element at times seems unreachable yet lies within the power of each of us. This element not only defines success but, in fact, is success. This element is when you can look into a mirror and say to yourself, "I like me." I like what I've achieved. I like what I stand for. I like who I am.

You may be thinking, "How can I like myself when I know I screw up and I'm not perfect?" Being successful isn't about not making mistakes or being perfect. We all have times in our lives when we wish we had made a different decision and achieved a different outcome. We are not perfect, and that is the point. Success is not about being perfect, it is about accepting yourself and all the ups and downs that make up your life. Life is like an impressionistic painting. When you stand too close to the painting, all you see are ugly blotches of light and dark color holding no meaning or form. As you step further back from the painting, the colors start to blend, and a recognizable picture emerges. It is this picture, seen in its totality, that is the definition of your life and the definition of your success. It is up to you to determine if your picture is to be dominated by the dark colors of disappointment and regret or the bright colors of pride and hope. You may not have control over the cards you were dealt, but you do have control over how you play them. If you play the cards in your life with integrity and take pride in the effort you put forth, then you will be able to say, "I like me, and I won the card game of life!"

Appendix

Commitment
Exercise 1: What Do I Value in Life?
Exercise 2: Value Comparison Inventory
Exercise 3: Finding Your Definition of Success
Exercise 4: Creating Your Mission Statement

Attitude
Exercise 5: Self-Affirmations
Exercise 6: Reframing for Success
Exercise 7: I Did It!
Exercise 8: Dealing with Nonsuccesses
Exercise 9: Creating Standards

Resources
Exercise 10: Know Your Skills
Exercise 11: Identifying Resources
Exercise 12: Identifying Human Resources

Decision Making
Exercise 13: Analyzing Decisions
Exercise 14: Decision Tree
Exercise 15: Decision Making: Plus-Minus-Implications
Exercise 16: ABCD of Problem Solving
Exercise 17: ACE Your Problems

Scheme
Exercise 18: Making a Winning Goal
Exercise 19: Analyzing Your Goal
Exercise 20: Webbing Your Goal
Exercise 21: Getting It Done
Exercise 22: Time Management

Classroom
Exercise 23: Find it in the CARDS
Exercise 24: Winning with CARDS in the Classroom
Exercise 25: Thirty Years from Now
Exercise 26: Life's Dilemmas

Exercise 1

What Do I Value in Life?

What we value defines who we are, how we behave and the direction we choose in our lives. For each value listed below indicate the level of importance to you.

Achievement: accomplishment; results brought about by resolve, persistence, or endeavor

      Not very Important   Important   Very Important

Aesthetic: the appreciation and enjoyment of beauty for beauty's sake, in the arts and nature

      Not very Important   Important   Very Important

Altruism: regard for or devotion to the interest of others; service to others

      Not very Important   Important   Very Important

Autonomy: the ability to be a self-determining individual; personal freedom, making own choices

      Not very Important   Important   Very Important

Creative: the creating of new ideas and designs; being innovative

      Not very Important   Important   Very Important

Emotional Well-Being: peace of mind, inner security; ability to recognize and handle inner conflicts

      Not very Important   Important   Very Important

Health: the condition of being sound in body

      Not very Important   Important   Very Important

Honesty: being frank and genuinely yourself with everyone

> Not very Important   Important   Very Important

Justice: treating others fairly or impartially; conforming to truth, fact or reason

> Not very Important   Important   Very Important

Knowledge: seeking truth, information, or principles for the satisfaction of curiosity

> Not very Important   Important   Very Important

Love: warmth, caring; unselfish devotion that freely accepts another in loyalty and seeks his good

> Not very Important   Important   Very Important

Loyalty: maintaining allegiance to a person, group, or individual

> Not very Important   Important   Very Important

Morality: believing and keeping ethical standards; personal honor, integrity

> Not very Important   Important   Very Important

Physical Appearance: concern for one's attractiveness; being neat, clean, well-groomed

> Not very Important   Important   Very Important

Pleasure: satisfaction, gratification, fun, joy

> Not very Important   Important   Very Important

Power: possession of control, authority, or influence over others

> Not very Important   Important   Very Important

Recognition: being important, well-liked, accepted

     Not very Important   Important   Very Important

Religious Faith: having a religious belief; being in relationship with God

     Not very Important   Important   Very Important

Skill: being able to use one's knowledge effectively; being good at doing something important to me and others

     Not very Important   Important   Very Important

Wealth: having many possessions and plenty of money for the things I want

     Not very Important   Important   Very Important

Wisdom: having mature understanding, insight, good sense, and judgement

     Not veryImportant   Important   Very Important

List below your top five values: List below your bottom five values:

_____   _____

_____   _____

_____   _____

_____   _____

_____   _____

Exercise 2

Value Comparison Inventory

It is one thing to say we know what we value, but it is another thing when those values come in conflict with one another. Such as the values of honesty versus loyalty when a friend is caught committing a crime and you are a witness. This exercise is designed to compare your values relative to one another and help reveal what you truly value.

Each item contains a group of characteristics. In each grouping rate the value you place on each characteristic. In front of the each characteristic place a number 1, for the characteristic you value the most in the grouping, to 5 in front of each characteristic you value least. Be careful to rate all characteristics in a group 1 through 5 and no ties please.

1. ( ) Justice
   ( ) Altruism
   ( ) Achievement
   ( ) Wealth
   ( ) Religious Faith

2. ( ) Altruism
   ( ) Recognition
   ( ) Autonomy
   ( ) Power
   ( ) Loyalty

3. ( ) Recognition
   ( ) Pleasure
   ( ) Wealth
   ( ) Love
   ( ) Creativity

4. ( ) Pleasure
   ( ) Wisdom
   ( ) Power
   ( ) Aesthetics
   ( ) Justice

8. ( ) Autonomy
   ( ) Wealth
   ( ) Health
   ( ) Emotional Well-Being
   ( ) Wisdom

9. ( ) Wealth
   ( ) Power
   ( ) Skill
   ( ) Knowledge
   ( ) Honesty

10. ( ) Power
    ( ) Love
    ( ) Emotional Well-Being
    ( ) Morality
    ( ) Achievement

11. ( ) Love
    ( ) Aesthetics
    ( ) Knowledge
    ( ) Religious Faith
    ( ) Autonomy

15. ( ) Skill
    ( ) Emotional Well-Being
    ( ) Creativity
    ( ) Altruism
    ( ) Aesthetics

16. ( ) Emotional Well-Being
    ( ) Knowledge
    ( ) Justice
    ( ) Recognition
    ( ) Physical Appearance

17. ( ) Knowledge
    ( ) Morality
    ( ) Altruism
    ( ) Pleasure
    ( ) Health

18. ( ) Morality
    ( ) Religious Faith
    ( ) Recognition
    ( ) Wisdom
    ( ) Skill

5. ( ) Wisdom
   ( ) Honesty
   ( ) Love
   ( ) Physical Appearance
   ( ) Altruism

12. ( ) Aesthetics
    ( ) Physical Appearance
    ( ) Morality
    ( ) Loyalty
    ( ) Wealth

19. ( ) Religious Faith
    ( ) Loyalty
    ( ) Pleasure
    ( ) Honesty
    ( ) Emotional Well-Being

6. ( ) Honesty
   ( ) Achievement
   ( ) Aesthetics
   ( ) Health
   ( ) Recognition

13. ( ) Physical Appearance
    ( ) Health
    ( ) Religious Faith
    ( ) Creativity
    ( ) Power

20. ( ) Loyalty
    ( ) Creativity
    ( ) Wisdom
    ( ) Achievement
    ( ) Knowledge

7. ( ) Achievement
   ( ) Autonomy
   ( ) Physical Appearance
   ( ) Skill
   ( ) Pleasure

14. ( ) Health
    ( ) Skill
    ( ) Loyalty
    ( ) Justice
    ( ) Love

21. ( ) Creativity
    ( ) Justice
    ( ) Honesty
    ( ) Autonomy
    ( ) Morality

Tabulating Value Comparison

To determine the relative strength of your values, record on this sheet the number you assigned, (1, 2, 3, 4, 5) to each value on the Value Comparison Inventory. Once you have completed this, add up the totals for each value. Then you are to assign a rank 1-21 starting with the lowest total as number 1 and the highest as 21.

							Totals	Rank
Achievement	——	——	——	——	——	——	——
Aesthetic	——	——	——	——	——	——	——
Altruism	——	——	——	——	——	——	——
Autonomy	——	——	——	——	——	——	——
Creative	——	——	——	——	——	——	——
Emotional Well-Being	——	——	——	——	——	——	——
Health	——	——	——	——	——	——	——
Honesty	——	——	——	——	——	——	——
Justice	——	——	——	——	——	——	——
Knowledge	——	——	——	——	——	——	——
Love	——	——	——	——	——	——	——
Loyalty	——	——	——	——	——	——	——
Morality	——	——	——	——	——	——	——
Physical Appearance	——	——	——	——	——	——	——
Pleasure	——	——	——	——	——	——	——

Power   ——   ——   ——   ——   ——   ——   ——

Recognition   ——   ——   ——   ——   ——   ——   ——

Religious Faith   ——   ——   ——   ——   ——   ——   ——

Skill   ——   ——   ——   ——   ——   ——   ——

Wealth   ——   ——   ——   ——   ——   ——   ——

Wisdom   ——   ——   ——   ——   ——   ——   ——

Exercise 3

Finding Your Definition of Success

Your personal definition of success can be found by analyzing your past successes. In this exercise you are to take three steps which will lead you to your definition for success.

Step 1: Using the Success History Form, write down times when you experienced success. The form has been broken down in age levels to help in your reflection on your past. Find three or more successes at each level if possible.

Step 2: Using the Why It's a Success form, identify what contributed to making you feel your success was a success. Then record the number of the statement on the Success History Form.

Step 3: Review which Why It's a Success statements appear most often on your Success History. Below are three boxes. In the first box below write the statements which appear most often on your record. In the second box, combine these statements and write your own unique definition of success.

Why It's a Success statements

I am successful when . . .

Success History Form

Write down three or more times when you experienced success at each age level.

Successes Ages 1-7	Why is it a success?
1.	
2.	
3.	
4.	

Successes Ages 7-12	Why is it a success?
1.	
2.	
3.	
4.	

Successes Ages 12-19	Why is it a success?
1.	
2.	
3.	
4.	

Successes Ages 12-19	Why is it a success?
1.	
2.	
3.	
4.	

Successes Ages 19-30	Why is it a success?
1.	
2.	
3.	
4.	

Successes Ages 30-45	Why is it a success?
1.	
2.	
3.	
4.	

Successes Ages 45-60	Why is it a success?
1.	
2.	
3.	
4.	

Successes Ages 60 and beyond	Why is it a success?
1.	
2.	
3.	
4.	

Why It's a Success

1. I used good insight and judgment.

2. I maintained or enhanced my own integrity, character and moral standards.

3. I accomplished something important.

4. I was free to decide what I did or how I did it.

5. I expressed love in a meaningful way.

6. I expressed my love for beauty.

7. I used skill and knowledge.

8. I did something for others or helped them do something important to them.

9. I did what was fair and just.

10. I met a challenge or had an adventure.

11. I persevered or enhanced my relationship to a person, group or institution.

12. I was creative.

13. I learned something I did not know before.

14. I received a great deal of personal pleasure.

15. I received respect, appreciation, recognition or approval.

16. I received money or its equivalent.

17. I increased my self respect.

18. I became more physically healthy.

19. I became more emotionally secure and /or fulfilled.

20. I became more influential and received greater opportunity to make thing happen.

Exercise 4

Creating Your Mission Statement

1. How would you like the people most important to you to describe you at your death? Write ten or more adjectives or phrases you would want them to say about you.

2. Choose the most important to you of the adjectives or phrases and identify what you must do to personify that description.

3. Finally, using the description of you and the behaviors or actions to achieve that description, write your own mission statement.

I want to be remembered as . . .	What I must do to achieve it:

My Mission Statement:

Exercise 5

Self-Affirmations

Throughout your day, stop and take the time to identify and write down three positive statements about yourself. Do this for twenty-one days and you will see your self-worth improve. Here are some examples to get you started:

- I really feel great
- I like people
- I deserve credit for trying
- My cooking sure tastes good
- I really handled that situation well
- I had fun with my friends today

- I'm considerate of others
- I'm a good person
- My boss is pleased with my work
- People like me
- I look good today
- My family is a source of happiness for me

Self-Monitoring Log Positive Statements

Date _____

Day _____

1. _____
2. _____
3. _____

Date _____

Day _____

1. _____
2. _____
3. _____

Date _____

Day _____

1. _____
2. _____
3. _____

Date _____

Day _____

1. _____
2. _____
3. _____

Date _____

Day _____

1. _____
2. _____
3. _____

Date _____

Day _____

1. _____

2. _____

3. _____

Date _____

Day _____

1. _____

2. _____

3. _____

Date _____

Day _____

1. _____

2. _____

3. _____

Date _____

Day _____

1. _____

2. _____

3. _____

Date _____

Day _____

1. _____

2. _____

3. _____

Exercise 6

Reframing for Success

Let's face it, bad things happen. The impact of bad things happening depends not so much on the incident as how you look at the incident. The defeated person sees the incident in terms of how they have failed and will never will. The successful person seeks out the positives of the situation and uses what happened to motivate themselves. For example, it is painful when a married couple breaks-up. There may be grieving over losing the person and the dreams you once had. You may be sad, angry, in denial, and wanting to barter your way back together. You may feel all of these feelings before you reach acceptance. Yet, how you see, or "frame" the situation will determine how you move on. If you see the break-up as an example of how you are a failure and that no one will ever love you then you will continue to be an unhappy person. But, if you "reframe" the situation and conclude: "We weren't a good fit and we are both better off being apart." "I deserve to be happy and find someone who is compatible." "We both changed and I learned much, moving on is part of life." A person who frames the break-up this way is able to move on with confidence and self-worth.

Below you will find a list of incidents followed the resulting thoughts framed in the negative. You are to write the positive reframing of the incident.

Incident	Negative Frame	Positive Frame
Example: *A flood destroyed my house.*	*I lost everything.*	*My family is safe. We can rebuild a house.*
I failed my driving test.	I will never be able to drive.	
I didn't get the raise I wanted.	They hate me. I'll never get a raise.	
I burned and ruined what I was cooking.	Cooking is too hard.	
My team lost.	We suck!	
I am second string	The coach hates me.	
I tripped on a curb, fell, and broke my leg.	Why does negative things always happen to me?	
The girl I asked out said no.	I will never get a date.	
I had to pay more taxes this year.	The government is out to destroy us.	

Exercise 7

I Did It!

The ancient pyramids were built carefully placing one block on top of another until the pyramid seemed to reach the sky. Those pyramids have lasted centuries due to the firm foundations each block was placed upon. Success is the culmination of carefully developed skills aligned just right. Just as each block in the pyramid was an engineering marvel in itself—so is each skill, each task, each bit of knowledge gained, each goal reached a success. The big successes in life are made up of smaller successes that hold up the big success. Without the smaller successes, there would be no big successes. It is therefore important to seek out and achieve the less dramatic or less recognized skills that will serve not only to increase our ability level but also our confidence level. With each success, no matter what the size, we grow in confidence that we can meet the next challenge, achieve the next goal.

As a means of increasing your confidence as well as your skill level make a list of your most memorable "I Did It" moments. It may have been tying your shoe for the first time, graduating from high school, or rebuilding a car. Those things that you achieved, that you mastered though your hard work and effort. Then keep another list of those things you achieved each day or each week, the "I Did It" moments in your life. If you can't identify many such moments, then maybe you are not appreciating what you can do or you need to take the risk to create such moments. You may want to identify a skill you want to master, a place you want to go or a person you want to meet and then, like the Nike slogan, "Just do it". Growing and learning is a risk taking proposition. Don't be afraid to take the risk because if you do you will reap the reward of being able to say, "**I Did It!**"

Examples
I Did It Moments in My Life

Learned to swim
Got hired at my first job
Overcame my fear and gave a speech in the seventh grade
Saved enough money to buy my first car
I figured fix my car when others couldn't

I Did It This Week

I passed a difficult Math test
I got up the courage to ask Jennifer out on a date
I beat Bill in the mile run
I learned how to download music on my ipod

Exercise 8

Dealing with Nonsuccesses

There is no such thing as failure—only "nonsuccesses". How we interpret the "nonsuccessful" moments in our lives has much to do with how we will respond. The reasons for our nonsuccess can lie internally, within our control or externally, outside of our control. It is important to understand the sources of the problem so we can design a plan of action that can turn a nonsuccess into a success. For example, when Michael did not make the varsity team there were possible internal and external reasons. Internally, football was a new sport to him and his lack of athletic skill and knowledge was a factor along with his being late to practice so often. The external causes, in addition to the other players being more skilled were that the coach knew the other players longer and had his favorites. By clearly identifying what he has control over in changing and what he has no control over Michael will be able to make a plan of action that can lead to success. One such plan for Michael may be to work harder in practice to improve his skill and to learn the plays, be on time to practice, and to take opportunities to show the coach he is dedicated to succeeding.

Below you are to write down a nonsuccess incident in your life. You are to then assess honestly your role in the nonsuccess and that of external forces. Then write what you will do to turn the non-success to a success.

Nonsuccess Incident

_____

_____

What were some of the internal causes?

_____

_____

What were some of the external causes?

_____

_____

Plan of Action

_____

_____

Exercise 9

Creating Standards

How we approach life and the actions we take depend upon what we believe. Those beliefs we acquire through growing up and the experiences we have and the people who influence us. By having clear beliefs from which to guide your life you will maintain a direction and purpose to your life. Often our beliefs and standards are expressed in a particular quotation or a stated list of standards. As a source of inspiration, direction and definition keep a running log of quotations, stories or statements that you identify with and feel are truths for your life. Here are a few to get you started:

> Dictionary is the only place that success comes before work—
> Vince Lombardi

Jefferson's Canons of Conduct
These rules of conduct were written by Thomas Jefferson in 1811 as instructions to his granddaughter, Cornelia, when she was twelve.

1. Never put off till tomorrow what you can do today.
2. Never trouble another with what you can do yourself.
3. Never spend your money before you have it.
4. Never buy a thing you do not want, because it is cheap, it will be dear to you.
5. Take care of your cents: Dollars with take care of themselves!
6. Pride costs us more than hunger, thirst, and cold.
7. We never repent of having eat too little.
8. Nothing is troublesome that one does willingly
9. How much pain have cost us the evils which have never happened.
10. Take things always by their smooth handle.
11. Think as you please, and so let others, and you will have no disputes.
14. When annoyed count 10, before you speak, if very angry, 100.

> Do what you can, with what you have, where you are.
> Theodore Roosevelt

> Help thy brother's boat across, and lo! Thine own has reached the shore.
> Hindu Proverb

> A man, as a general rule, owes very little to what
> he is born with—a man is what he makes of himself.
> Alexander Graham Bell

Exercise 10

Know Your Skills

Below is a list of skills. Rate yourself on a scale of one to five. Refer to the scale below as you rate your strengths and weaknesses.

1. Strength
2. Good Skills
3. So-So Skills
4. Below Average Skills
5. Weak or non-existent Skills

SKILLS	**RATING**
1. Cooking	_____
2. Home Repair	_____
3. Keeping a clean home	_____
4. General organization	_____
5. Budgeting your money	_____
6. Home decorating	_____
7. Taking care of children	_____
8. Reading	_____
9. Sports	_____
10. Playing a musical instrument	_____
11. Singing	_____
12. Painting or drawing	_____
13. Acting	_____
14. Crafts & woodworking	_____
15. Oral communication with others	_____
16. Written communication with others	_____
17. Public speaking	_____
18. Listening	_____
19. Understanding others feelings	_____
20. Working in a group	_____
21. Making others laugh	_____
22. Selling a product or idea	_____
23. Managing others	_____
24. Organization	_____
25. Motivating others	_____
26. Computer	_____

27. Working with numbers   _____
28. Following orders exactly   _____
29. Taking initiative   _____
30. Working alone   _____
31. Teaching or presenting ideas or information   _____
32. Taking risks   _____
33. Driving a car   _____
34. Solving mechanical problems   _____
35. Solving social problems   _____
36. Taking tests   _____
37. Writing essays   _____
38. Taking notes in class   _____
39. Memory   _____
40. Auto repair   _____
41. Sewing   _____
42. Working with animals   _____
43. Gardening   _____
44. Large construction; houses, landscape   _____
45. Making others happy   _____

Now review your list and circle your ten greatest strengths and then rank those from one to ten in importance to you. After doing that then put a check mark next to the skills that you would like to improve.

Exercise 11

Identifying Resources

It is one thing to be able to identify the resources you need to achieve a goal, but it is another to find a way to succeed with the resources you have. This exercise is designed to help you to get practice doing both. First is presented a list of goals and you are to identify five resources you might find useful in reaching the goal. You can use the list of resources provided more than once, but for each goal identify at least one resource not on the list. Second is presented a list of problems with the resources available to you. You are to rank the value of each resource in solving your problem.

Resources: bank, blender, calorie book, compass, computer, hammer, internet, large cooking pot, map, measuring cups, measuring tape, music, newspaper, radio, refrigerator, running shoes, scissors, shovel, shrub clippers, thesaurus, vacuum cleaner, wrench,

Going to College:

1._____ 2._____ 3._____ 4._____ 5._____

Loosing weight

1._____ 2._____ 3._____ 4._____ 5._____

Traveling to Europe

1._____ 2._____ 3._____ 4._____ 5._____

Hosting a dinner party at your home for twenty-five people

1._____ 2._____ 3._____ 4._____ 5._____

Redesigning your back yard

1._____ 2._____ 3._____ 4._____ 5._____

You are lost in a large city in a foreign country and you do not speak the language. Rank the following resources as to their importance to helping you find your way to your hotel.

___ candy bar   ___ picture of the hotel   ___ country map   ___ water
___ binoculars   ___ USA cell phone   ___ airline ticket   ___ watch
___ ipod   ___ compass   ___ camera   ___ sun glasses
___ your hometown news paper

At 9:00 pm gas and electricity service has been interrupted in your neighborhood due to a transformer fire at the electric company. Rank the following resources as to their importance in getting you through three days without these services.

___ TV set   ___ candles   ___ oven   ___ blankets
___ bananas   ___ pliers   ___ deck of cards   ___ computer
___ matches   ___ bottled water   ___ Barbeque   ___ cereal
___ transistor radio

Exercise 12

Identifying Human Resources

A hammer is a resource. It is a tool with a definite purpose that can be applied to different situations but for basically one purpose, to pound something. Objects are generally limited to the purpose for which they were designed. Yes, they can be used in creative ways to establish a new purpose but generally they are limited in the functions object can perform. People are the opposite. They are resources that pocess multiple skills that can be applied to unlimited purposes. It is therefore important to not only to label a person a resource but to also understand how they can help you.

Below you are to identify four people in your world and list the skills, talents and connections they have that may prove to be useful to you in reaching future goals. Use the example to get started.

Example

Name of Person: *Uncle Hairy*		
General contractor	*Plays golf often*	*Best fried owns auto repair*
Likes cooking	*Generous*	*Good listener*

Name of Person:		

Name of Person:		

Name of Person:		

Name of Person:		

Exercise 13

Analyzing Decisions

One of the simplest ways of analyzing a decision is to list the advantages and disadvantages of the choices. After doing this, you can assign a value to each item you wrote down in a number of different ways. (A) You can use a rating system of "High", "Medium", or "Low" to determine the importance of each item. (B) You can give a numerical ranking of importance to each item. You may find that while a list is shorter, it may contain the most important items as identified by the rankings, (C) You can give a value to each item of one (least valuable) through ten (most valuable). You then add up the numbers to determine which column of items is the most valued.

What would you like to do?

_____

_____

Advantages	value	Disadvantages	value
Total		Total	

Based on your analysis, does your choice have more advantages or more disadvantages? Is it a good decision? Explain.

_____

_____

Exercise 14

Decision Tree

A "Decision Tree" can be a great way to visualize the relationship between the problem, possible solutions, and consequences. On the trunk of the tree below write down the problem or dilemma you are facing. On each of the limbs of the tree write down all of your options or actions you could take to solve the problem. On the leaves of each limb write down the possible outcomes if you were to choose the solution stated on the limb. Add more limbs and leaves as needed. Finally step back and analyze which of the solutions would result in the best outcome.

Exercise 15

Decision Making: Plus-Minus Implication

In this method of decision making you are going to focus more on the impact of each advantage or disadvantage involved in your decision. You will being this exercise by writing down a decision that you are thinking about making. Under the "Plus" column, write the positive results of your action. Under the "Minus" column, list the negative effects. Under "Implications" you write the possible outcomes both positive and negative. You can assign point values to each of the items listed, giving positive points to the plus column, negative points to each item in the minus column and positive or negative points to the implications.

Decision:

_____

_____

Plus	Minus	Implications

Analyze your chart above. Will your decision have a positive or negative impact?

_____

_____

Exercise 16

A-B-C-D of Problem Solving

Many people feel like victims to their problems because they don't take the time to understand what lead up to the problem. They don't analyze the course of events they and others took that resulted in things not working out. By answering four simple questions, you can gain a greater understanding of a problem you had, your response to it, and what you could decide to do to solve the problem in the future. You can also use these same four questions to analyze your options before you act. Just identify what is the issue as the activating event, list what behaviors you could do, the consequences of those behaviors and then decide which behavior is your best course of action. It can be as easy as A-B-C-D.

A—Activating Event: What is the activating event that started the problem?

B—Behavior: What was your behavior or that of others involved?

C—Consequences: What were the consequences of your behavior to you and others?

D—Decision: What do you decide to do differently in the future?

Exercise 17

ACE Your Problems

The most valuable card in a deck of cards is the Ace. If you are having trouble identifying your options to solving a problem, you only have to remember ACE.

All problems or situations no matter how small or complex have only three possible solutions. You can **adapt** or adjust to the situation, you can **change** the situation, or you can **escape** from the situation. Adapt, Change or Escape—ACE. The details of what you do may vary with the problem you are facing but whatever action you take, it will be characterized by one of these three choices. For example, let's say you had a boss that frequently blew up and put pressure on those around him, including you. You could choose to adapt by "tuning" your boss out so you don't hear him as much or exercising frequently to burn off the frustration you are feeling. You could try to change your boss by talking with him about how you could help him to be less angry and frustrated. Or, you could escape the pressure by looking for another job. As you can see there may be many different approaches to adapting to or changing a situation. You may try one approach such as changing the situation only to come to the realization that you have to adapt to it because it can't be changed and you can't afford to escape by leaving your job due to finances and obligations. Deciding what to do depends upon identifying your options, testing them out and adjusting based upon what you have learned.

Think of a problem or situation that you or someone else has that requires something to be done. Write down the problem and then list all the actions or steps you could take to adapt, change or escape the situation. Finally decide on which is the best course of action to try first.

What is the problem? _____

_____

What can you do to **adapt** to the problem? _____

_____

_____

_____

_____

What can you do to **change** the problem? _____

_____

_____

_____

_____

_____

What can you do to **escape** the problem? _____

_____

_____

_____

_____

_____

Exercise 18

Making a Winning Goal

Everyone sets goals in their life, but successful people know how to set winning goals. Many times we set goals that have the potential to fail before we ever get started. Ask yourself if the following five ingredients are present in your goal. If they are, then you have a goal that has the potential to succeed.

1. Is your goal **Definable?** Put your goal into words that are understandable and will identify the first step and each step to follow.
2. Is your goal **Achievable?** Is the goal something that lies within your given strengths and abilities?
3. Is your goal **Desirable?** Is the goal something that you really want to achieve, not something that you feel forced to do? Joy and motivation comes from that which we value.
4. Is your goal **Measurable?** Have you stated when, or how long, or what quantity is necessary for you to achieve your goal? If you can not measure your goal then how do you know when you achieved it?
5. Is your goal **Controllable?** Do you have power over everything and everyone in your stated goal? If success depends upon someone else doing something, then failure is a possibility out of your control.

Write a goal that you would like to achieve by answering the following questions.

My goal is defined as _____
_____
_____
_____

My goal is achievable because _____
_____
_____
_____

My goal is desirable because _____
_____
_____
_____

My goal is measurable by _____

_____

_____

_____

My goal is controllable because _____

_____

_____

_____

Now state a winning goal using what you have identified above.

I will _____

_____

_____

_____

Exercise 19

Analyzing Your Goal

1. What is your short-range goal? _____
   _____
   _____
   _____

2. How soon, realistically, would you like to achieve your goal? _____
   _____
   _____
   _____

3. What present strengths do you possess that will help you achieve this goal?
   _____
   _____
   _____

4. What new strengths might be required to achieve this goal?
   _____
   _____
   _____

5. What makes this goal desirable to you? _____
   _____
   _____
   _____

6. What barriers, if any, do you anticipate that might keep you from achieving your goal? _____
   _____
   _____
   _____

7. Suggest three ways in which you might manage each barrier and the resources needed to help you achieve the goal.

BARRIER   SOLUTIONS & RESOURCES

—————————   1.————————————————————————
            2.————————————————————————
            3.————————————————————————

—————————   1.————————————————————————
            2.————————————————————————
            3.————————————————————————

—————————   1.————————————————————————
            2.————————————————————————
            3.————————————————————————

—————————   1.————————————————————————
            2.————————————————————————
            3.————————————————————————

—————————   1.————————————————————————
            2.————————————————————————
            3.————————————————————————

Exercise 20

Webbing A Goal

Before writing a formal step-by-step plan to achieving a goal, it often helps to brainstorm and visualize what will go into accomplishing the goal seeing how one thing leads and relates to the next. Start by writing down your goal in the middle of the page and circle it. Then from the circle make a line for each idea, thought, need or component of the goal that comes to your mind. Then from each of the items you wrote, write what comes to mind related to that word. You can continue this process for as long as is practical. Then look at the web you have created and connect any items which may be related or the same. Finally, from your web create a sequential "to-do" list to reach your goal.

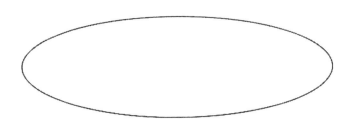

Exercise 21

Getting It Done

Having a goal is the first step, but you will be standing in place if you don't devise a plan for getting it done. In fact you don't set one goal, you actually set a series of goals that have to be reached before you achieve your final goal. By breaking down your scheme into these shorter and simpler goals you make your task more manageable and achievable. In addition, completing each step gives you a sense of progress which fuels your motivation to go on.

After setting your primary goal, walk backwards in your mind and on paper answering the question, "What has to be done before I reach this point." With each point you establish ask the same question and write down your answer. Continue this process until you reach where you are starting from, where you are right now. After writing down your steps, start at the bottom of the list and work your way up towards your goal by completing each task along the way.

Primary Goal: _____

Step before: _____

Step before: _____

Step before: _____

Step before: _____

Step before: _____

Step before: _____

Step before: _____

Step before: _____

Step before: _____

Step before: _____

Exercise 22

Time Management

Does it seem like you are always running out of time to get things done, or there is too much to do, or you can't get the drive to do it? While these are common complaints, you will have to overcome them if you are to be successful in managing your time.

There are four factors to consider as you prepare to manage the tasks before you.

1. What do you have to do?
2. How important is it?
3. How much time do you have?
4. How motivating is the task?

Without a scheme that addresses these factors you may find yourself spinning your wheels and getting burned-out. The key to good health is balance, and it is important to balance these factors in constructing your daily, weekly and monthly schedule.

What to do: Start by making a "To Do List" putting on it everything you need and would like to get done. You can make the list as detailed as you would like. You may want to break some tasks down into smaller parts to make the task clearer and less imposing.

How important is it: Not all tasks have an equal importance or require equal effort. By using the diagram below, decide where each item on your To Do List would fall in terms of priority and effort.

High Impact/ Low Effort	High Impact/ High Effort
Low Impact/ Low Effort	Low Impact/ High Effort

How much time: Decide how much time you have in your work day. Then estimate how much time each item on your To Do List will take to complete. In selecting which items you will complete remember "you can't fit a ten pounds in a five pound bag".

How motivating is it: Not everything we have to do is fun and rewarding. If we are faced with draining, unrewarding tasks all day our motivation and energy level will shrink along with out productivity. Looking back at the importance chart above, combine activities so that some low effort activities will balance the more high effort ones. If do to the high priority of the task you find yourself putting out high effort for prolonged periods of time, balance it with down time to relax and recharge your batteries.

Time Management Worksheet

List what to do. Then rate the impact (high/low), the effort (high/low), the time to complete, and your motivation to complete it (high/low). After analyzing the chart, identify a balanced scheme for your day, week, or month.

To Do List	Time	Impact	Effort	Motivation

Tasks and the order of the tasks I will complete from to   .

Exercise 23

Find it in the CARDS

Read one of the stories from the Journeys to Success section of *Winning at the Card Game of Life* and answer the following questions.

Journey of _____

- What was the primary **commitment** or passion of the person?

- What are examples of the **attitude** that contributed to them being successful?

- What **resources** contributed to the person's success?

- What **decisions** did the person make that lead to their success?

- What was the **scheme** the person followed to become successful?

Exercise 24

Winning with CARDS in the Classroom

Name _____ Class _____ Date_____

As you prepare for this class, use CARDS to analyze what you will need to do to succeed.

- **Commitment:** What is the grade you wish to achieve and from a low of one to a high of ten, how much effort are you committed to giving to the class?

- **Attitude:** What attitude, standards and systems of self-discipline will you use to succeed?

- **Resources:** What resources will you use to get the grade you desire?

- **Decisions:** What decisions will you have to make in regards to how you spend your time, and what actions and sacrifices must you make to be successful?

- **Scheme:** What plan or routine will you follow to be successful in this class?

Exercise 25

Thirty Years from Now

Imagine that it is thirty years from now and you are reflecting upon the successful life you have enjoyed. Visualize and answer the questions: Where you are living and what does it look like? What post high school training or schooling did you complete? What did you accomplish in your career? Did you get married? Did you have children and if so how many? Make the visualization of life as detailed as possible. Next answer the following using CARDS.

- What was your primary **commitment** or passion?

- What are examples of the **attitude** that contributed to your being successful?

- What **resources** contributed to your success?

- What **decisions** did you make that lead to your success?

- What was the **scheme** that you followed to become successful?

Exercise 26

Life's Dilemmas

1. A young store clerk of a large chain store gives you $20.00 too much in change on a high priced item. What do you do?

2. Your boss is being very degrading and rude to a fellow employee who is a close friend of yours. What do you do?

3. You spent hours decorating you apartment and feel proud about how it looks, only to return home to find that your roommate changed it and she is very excited about how it now looks. What do you do?

4. Your best friend was unable to study for the final and tells you if he can't copy off your answer sheet he will fail. What do you do?

5. Your car was badly scraped up in a parking lot and your insurance deductible is too high to cover getting it fixed. It will cost 80% of your savings to get it looking nice again. What do you do?

6. The group that you have been trying to get accepted into finally asked you to come with them to a party, but you have a major test the next day that you will fail and the class as well if you don't study. What do you do?

7. A very important client who you have been trying to sign to a deal calls you to say that he can meet with you only at 7:00 tonight, the same time of your daughter's one performance play at school. What do you do?

8. You are offered a promotion which means a 25% increase in your salary but you have to re-locate 1500 miles away from the town where all of your family and friends live. What do you do?

9. A member of a group is being denied the attention of the group to express his point of view. You agree with the position of the group and you are running out of time, but you have always said it is important that everyone has a chance to express themselves. What do you do?

References

Duckworth, Angela and Martin Seligman. "Self-Discipline Outdoes IQ in Predicting Academic Performance of Adolescents." *American Psychological Society* 16, no. 12 (2005).

Frankl, Victor. *Man's Search for Meaning.* New York: Washington Square Press, 1946

Goldstein, Arnold and Glick, Barry, *Aggression Replacement Training.* Champaign: Research Press, 1987.

Gore, Al. *The Assault on Reason.* New York: The Penguin Press, 2007. p. 254

Katz, Mark. *On Playing a Poor Hand Well.* New York: W.W. Norton & Company, 1997

Exercise 1 and 2 were found in the Achievement Motivation Program that was developed in 1971 through Combined Motivation Education Systems. Attempts to contact the creators of the exercises to get permission to republish led to W. Clement and Jessie V. Stone Foundation. No record of this exercise was found by the foundation personnel.

Please note that none of the individuals whose stories appear in this book were ever patients of Dr. McGlenn.

Dr. Bob McGlenn
Psychologist/Author

Dr. Bob McGlenn is a clinical and school psychologist who, in addition to maintaining a private practice since 1977, has experience in a variety of mental health areas. He has worked as a school psychologist at both the elementary and secondary levels, trained and supervised doctoral level interns at area psychiatric hospitals and community-based clinics, and consulted with a residential treatment center for severely disturbed adolescents. Dr. McGlenn designed and directed the implementation of the crisis response plan to the Santana and Granite Hills high schools shootings in March 2001. He designed and coordinated the Santana Recovery Project, which provided services and treatment to those traumatized by the event. Since the incident, he has spoken to numerous groups concerning school safety and has worked for the National School Safety Center as a trainer for the Community Oriented Policing Services program (COPS) and as a consultant to the Department of Homeland Security. In addition, Dr. McGlenn gives presentations on "The Keys to Successful Parenting" and "Winning at the Card Game of Life."

Despite having been very successful in his professional life, Dr. McGlenn feels that his greatest success is the love and happiness he experiences in his family. He and Diana have been married since 1977 and have three children, Jennifer, Matthew, and Michael.

Success depends not upon the cards you were dealt,
but rather how you play them.